Pauline

A MEMOIR

PAULINE HAND

WITH
DEBORAH MORGAN & ABIGAIL HORNE

Contents

Dedication

Grand, we never did finish your book, yet somehow, here you are, exactly where you belong, cherished in Nan's.

We did it.

Introduction

Beautifully captured in a series of personal recollections, my family and I have reflected together on the cherished family memories of more than eighty years.

To gift ourselves a treasure like no other, over just a few short months, we have been able to bring this wonderful book to life as a result of all the precious conversations that these pages will uncover.

Owning a book publishing company, Authors & Co, I know all too well that capturing the memories of a loved one in book form is one of the most precious gifts that you can ever give to yourself and others. So, with that said, we have published a memoir lovingly curated by three generations, my Grandmother *(Pauline)*, my Mother *(Deborah)* & I *(Abigail)*.

This Memoir is filled with a love that will last beyond any lifetime, and is a legacy for the future generations of our family.

We hope that this inspires you and wish you all the love and joy in the world as we encourage you to create your own legacy with your loved ones.

Abigail

My Paternal Grandparents

M y paternal grandparents, Matthew Owen and Mary Louisa Owen (née Edwards) lived in a little house in Dresden, Staffordshire. Grandma Owen died before I was born, but I knew Grandad Owen as a lovely, kind man. He gave me a brass box he had brought home from the First World War, that I still treasure today. It had an emblem of the King's head on it and contained chocolate and cigarettes. Those boxes were very popular and well known at the time, as every soldier from that war received one from the King. My Grandad Owen brought two back, so he also gave one to my cousin Maureen.

Grandad and Grandma Owen had a lot of children. Sadly, their first few died, which wasn't uncommon in that era, with now-preventable deaths caused by illnesses like pneumonia being rife in those days. With my grandparents' family, it's quite shocking to see the difference between the censuses taken ten years apart, their first lot of children having disappeared from one census to another. This meant I only got to know the children they had later, who grew up to be my loving aunties and uncles.

Grandma Owen died of ovarian cancer and bowel cancer when my dad was just sixteen. So, my dad's sister, Auntie Polly, stepped up to look after her younger siblings, with Dad as the youngest.

My Maternal Grandparents

M y grandad, William Henry Jenkins, fought in the First World War in a British regiment attached to the Indian Army. As Grandad Jenkins wasn't based in Europe during the war, it would have been too difficult to travel home and, therefore, he took all his leave in Delhi, India. The silver lining was that he returned with some unique gifts for Grandma and my mum, such as silks to make dresses and a beautiful broach which he watched being handmade on the side of the road. I still have that broach, which has a butterfly with gold threads and jet gemstones. He also brought back an ivory crochet hook for Grandma, which I still have somewhere, too.

I fondly remember my grandma, Mary Lizzie Jenkins (née Birks). Sadly, however, Grandma and Grandad Jenkins died young of industrial diseases. But I will tell you more about that later.

My Parents and Uncle Dennis

❧

My parents, Alec Owen and Hilda Owen (née Jenkins) were born-again Christians. I know they met at a dance, but they didn't really talk about it. In the 1930s they attended the 'crusades' and at one of their bonfires, they burnt their dancing shoes on the fire as a declaration that they wanted to dedicate their lives to God and live a life of service to Him.

I was an only child when I came along in 1940, as Mum lost a baby before me. She never had another child, probably because she had me at twenty-seven, which was old in those days, and during the war there was no time or opportunity for having babies, with husbands away on duty.

I got on very well with my parents and was very much loved by them. My mother, Hilda, was lovely, gorgeous, and a wonderful mum, and latterly a wonderful grandmother. She was very maternal, loving and caring, always making clothes for me. She was very different from my maternal grandmother, who, lovely as she was, had been very fashionable but not quite so maternal. My parents were so good to me and we never had an argument or raised angry voices. So, I'm thankful for having grown up in a loving home with a serene atmosphere, in a family that couldn't have had more love.

The story of my early years can't be told without introducing you to Uncle Dennis, my mum's brother, as there was never a time that Dennis wasn't there. Dennis was Grandma Jenkins'

son who came along very late in life, in 1932. For context, Roy, Grandma Jenkins' grandson, was older than Dennis! We have a photo of them all together which I will share with you.

Due to my grandparents' age and poor health, they were not well enough to look after Dennis, so he came to live with us. My mother brought him up even though he was her little brother, as she was twenty years his senior.

My mother adored Dennis, but she had quite a hard time with him as he could be difficult. At the time, they said he was 'backward', as he couldn't read or write, and they gave him comics to look at in school. Of course, we now understand he must have had learning difficulties.

My mother used to do everything for him and was simply marvellous with him, dealing with all his correspondence. I remember how she used to say, 'I am Dennis' secretary.' We thought she loved him more than any living thing! My dad was good with Dennis, too, which was helpful as not many husbands would have put up with that situation in those days. But my dad just wanted to make my mum happy, even when Dennis could sometimes be quite a cheeky monkey with his behaviour, often bringing new girlfriends home. Even so, he was lovely and very much loved by the whole family.

As I didn't have any siblings, I was happy to grow up with Uncle Dennis as a brother figure and we remained very close throughout our lives.

Early Days of the Second World War

$\curlywedge$

I was born in 1940 during the Second World War, so my early memories are very much defined by what it was like to grow up in the war days.

As my dad was in the Territorial Army before the Second World War, he was called up ahead of many others in the months before the war started.

He began in the King Shropshire Light Infantry, which he called the 'KSLI', but when they came to check his regiment, which was due to go overseas, Dad was pulled out for being too short, at only five feet and two inches. He was transferred to a guard regiment in the Royal Welsh Fusiliers, which inadvertently saved his life. The KSLI Regiment were all killed on the ship that he would have boarded, which I believe sank due to an accident. I don't know what they were doing, but there were lots of projects going on during the war that we didn't know about. Tragically, many of his friends went down on that boat. It was such a close call for Dad that, even though he hadn't been on board, the administration hadn't caught up with the events of his transfer, so his name appeared on the Roll of Honour as if he had been killed!

Dad's brothers were also part of the Pentecostal Church and were conscientious objectors during the war. Being devout Christians, they didn't agree with killing others. Even though my parents were part of the same church, my dad believed very firmly he should fight for his country. Though he always respected the opinion of his very dear brothers.

My dad was stationed in various places such as Jersey, North Wales, Kent, and the Isle of Man. He didn't like going to the Isle of Man though; he had the worst boat trip of his life there because of the choppy waters in the Irish Sea. But he liked Herne Bay very much, down on the Kent coast, where they had been expecting the Germans to arrive across the Channel (the Germans never came). My father also guarded the Menai Bridge, on the straight in North Wales, that takes you over to Anglesey.

With Dad stationed in Wales quite a lot, Mum and I went to live in Llandudno, Wales, so that my dad could take his leave there. It worked well as I had an auntie living there, so we spent six years living with Auntie Emmie, more or less until the war ended in 1945. We loved it so much that we returned to Llandudno for all our holidays after the war.

I have quite a lot of pictures of our time in Llandudno, some printed in this book, starting from 1943 when I would have been only three years old.

Auntie Emmie and Uncle Tom

Auntie Emmie was from Stoke-on-Trent originally. She was brought up as Mum's sister even though she was a cousin (on Grandma Jenkins' side). As a little girl, she had turned up at my grandparents' house in the middle of the night with her brother and sister, after her stepmother had thrown them out. In those days, if your mother died and your father remarried, it wasn't uncommon to be left on the street by your stepmother. Grandma Jenkins took them in and raised her nieces and nephew as her own. She was marvellous with them, and they were all very happy and close.

When Auntie Emmie was thirteen, she went into service as a maid in a big house in Llandudno on the North Wales coast, along with her sister and her best friend. She met her husband there, Uncle Tom, who was a Welshman and Welsh-speaking, too. She had a marvellous life there and she ended up spending her life in Llandudno.

We loved her so much. She was always making lots of jokes, with a cheeky side to her character. She was always good fun!

Auntie Emmie worked at the Palladium cinema as an usherette, showing people to their seats. Interestingly, that building has now become Llandudno's big Weatherspoon pub! Living in a seaside town, Uncle Tom and Auntie Emmie had a lot of jobs. As well as being an usherette, Auntie Emmie was also a cleaner. Uncle Tom, when not on duty in the war, used to drive a bus for mystery tours that travelled around the North Wales coast. Once, he did a mystery tour and brought them to Trentham Gardens, so he brought Auntie Emmie with him and dropped her off at our house in Dresden. He also worked at the tip.

Uncle Tom had a very difficult war and saw a lot of action. He was at the D-Day landings in 1944 and he also marched into Germany. He never talked about it, though my Dad always said he was a proper war hero. As he was abroad throughout the war, he couldn't make it home during any leave. This meant my mum and Auntie Emmie were important company for each other. Mrs Lathem, my mum's next door neighbour back home in Dresden, and her son Derek, also came to Llandudno to stay with us for weeks at a time. This meant there were often three families in that flat, but it was quite a spacious apartment above a shop on Mostyn Street. The apartment was rented because in those days very few people we knew owned their homes – my parents, for example, rented their house from a private landlord throughout their lives.

The War Years Continue

~

I t was hard growing up during the war. We had to carry gas masks everywhere, in a square tin case worn around our neck like a crossbody bag. Mothers carried young children's masks and were instructed how to fit the mask if needed, a little like when you go on an aeroplane now. I hated putting my gas mask on because it covered my whole head and really frightened me. Each time I did it, I was reminded of going to the dentist (in those days dentists would give you gas, covering your face with a mask). I screamed and cried when I had my mask fitted, despite the Mickey Mouse designs they cleverly used for children's masks. In the end, my mum said to leave it as it was just scaring me to death.

The air raid shelters were also frightening. Although, luckily, we didn't have shelters in Llandudno as we lived in flats. We may have had a different type of war in Llandudno than in the

Midlands, being on the north coast of Wales, perhaps with lower risks of air raids.

War life was a different story when we visited our home on Churchfield Avenue, in Stoke-on-Trent, usually for around two weeks at a time. There, the Germans once dropped a bomb on the Meir Aerodrome, close to our home.

We knew the Germans were coming in their aeroplanes whenever we heard the sirens blaring. My mum and I would rush into the garden and scramble down a few steps into the shelter with our gas masks on. I remember being frightened, not wanting to go down, and not wanting to put my mask on despite my mum's efforts.

We had a horrible Anderson shelter made of corrugated tin and buried in the garden, camouflaged with moss and plants growing over the tin roof. They were only built for six people, so they weren't terribly spacious, and I remember having to remain seated in our shelter, despite the water seeping through the soil and into my clothes. There were also often frogs and creepy crawlies who had made a home in the moist abode. To this day, I am still frightened of frogs. My mum was afraid of the creepy crawlies, too. In fact, she feared many things – even lighting and thunder – so the war experience must have been petrifying for her.

One of our neighbours in Churchfield Avenue, Mr Trevers, was the local warden. He tried cajoling my mum into the shelter, but she was terrified, so we often took cover under the table or our bed instead. After several air raids, I remember Mum saying,

'Look, we'll lie in the bed and if we're bombed, we're bombed. That's too bad.'

We were that frightened of those frogs and creepy crawlies!

My mum was also scared of cows and there is a funny story that deserves a mention. When I was really young and we were staying at home in Stoke-on-Trent, Mum used to do Grandma's washing and ironing due to her poorly chest. To do the washing, Mum and I would have to cross the fields and transport all the laundry in a basket for two to three miles, twice a week. One day, we had to go across a field full of cows. Upon seeing how many cows there were, Mum got a fright and sat me on the laundry before running off and leaving me!

Dad didn't get leave from duty very often, so when he came home, either to Llandudno or Stoke-on-Trent, it was a joyous time. Those were the memorable and special moments for me in the war days. One time, he was so desperate to see my mum that he walked from Shrewsbury to Stoke-on-Trent because there was no transport available! That's forty-odd miles – quite an impressive show of affection – especially during the war. To put that distance into context, my daughter Deborah now has a static caravan just outside Shrewsbury and it takes over an hour to get there by car, so imagine doing it by foot.

Mum was very happy to spend time with my dad when he was on leave. She was always missing him so much. And even though we wouldn't necessarily do anything special, as we didn't have much money, it was just perfect. We lived day by day, spending time together in the best way we could.

Something that sticks in my memory is how at the end of his leave, I used to see my dad off on the train. For those occasions, I used to bring the cats with me in a pram or a carrier bag, dressed in hats and doll's dresses. Thinking of it now, I bet the cats hated it! The station was always busy with soldiers leaving their loved ones, and lots of tears were shed as no one ever knew if their loved ones would return. They were very scary times and so many people lost their lives.

In my immediate family, there were some near misses and tragedies that affected different family members. Grandma Jenkins, for example, was working as a supervisor in a factory not far from Stoke-on-Trent, in Swynnerton, where they made munitions. The factory itself was a dangerous place to work, being a target for air raids. Grandma also lost a friend there when she was killed in an accidental explosion. I remember how she carried a photograph of her friend in her handbag all the time. We still have Grandma's bag today, filled with things like hairclips that she confiscated from the workers as they were contraband items.

The next story isn't from the war days as such, but I was reminded of it when recalling the near misses we had in our family because of the war. In the 1980s, my late husband Ted's cousin and her husband, Margaret and Ray, were doing some decorating in the house, knocking on a chimney breast, when they found an unexploded bomb from the Second World War. They were photographed for the local paper, the Evening Sentinel, holding this unexploded bomb!

The war years were bleak for many people. Even if you didn't lose someone directly, grief was all around you. I used to stay with my Auntie Polly sometimes, and one day, while I was there, her neighbour, Mrs Pointon, found out that her husband had been killed. The sadness I witnessed that day will stay with me forever. It was a real tragedy because Mrs Pointon's daughter then died of meningitis not long after. They buried them within a short time of one another.

It was very hard for children growing up in the war days, with fear and poverty a part of daily life. But it was the simple things, which we take for granted now, like basic toys, that we didn't have. But children will be children, and we adapted, being innately inventive, playing indoor games like Ludo and Snakes and Ladders (remembering there was no television!). We also played outside with a skipping rope or entertained ourselves by making 'telephones' with cocoa tins tied together at the end of a string. With one tin through one window and the second tin in another, or even across the street, we would pull the rope really tight before having conversations from one side to another. You could hear everything, amazingly; it was just like having a telephone. My mum was also brilliant at finding ways of making something out of nothing. She used to buy me newborn chickens to play with. It was awful come to think of it because they often died. But it was the war days and we were just doing our best to adapt and live our lives the best way we could, day by day, without much money.

Grandma Jenkins was creative, too. In the 1940s, dolls were scary looking things without pretty clothes or smiling faces. So,

Grandma used to crochet clothes and make doll's dresses. This meant there were always other people's dolls sitting in the corner of the room without clothes on, waiting in line for Grandma to make them an outfit. At Christmas, there were half a dozen dolls in her house that needed dressing, and Grandma would say, 'Don't touch those dolls, they are not yours!'

Dolls were difficult to get hold of during the war and I hankered for one. One day, while I was out with Auntie Emmie, we found a black doll in a shop that had a black leather body, arms, and legs. There is a photograph of me clutching that doll and crying because I wanted her so much. My Auntie Emmie kindly bought the doll for me. She often bought me things, as even though she had a son, Derek, she loved little girls. Perhaps that's why she thought the world of me. I loved her very much.

The doll became my prized possession, filling hours of my play-time until I dropped it and smashed its head! Thankfully, we took it to the 'doll's hospital' in Fenton, where a new head was fixed on. I was relieved to have my doll back, but it was never quite the same after having a new head. Nonetheless, I was a lucky girl, and I never took my toys for granted. I still have that doll which is now eighty years old.

Rationing

ᚲᚱᚹᚢ

Food was scarce throughout the war days, exacerbating the harshness of daily life, but we made do with what we had. I had my portion of sweets with the sweet coupons in the ration book, and when I went to the pictures with my mother, we could get two ounces of sweets. It wasn't much, but it was what we knew.

Mum always tried to get whatever food she could. Being a beautiful cook, she could make a good meal out of anything. Her lobby and her joint of lamb on a Sunday were my favourites. Lamb was important in our family, and in later years, I remember Auntie Emmie's house was always filled with the smell of lamb cooking on Saturday nights, ready for our family dinners on Sunday. It was always delicious having a taster of the lamb on Saturday evenings with Auntie Emmie's 'doorstep' sandwiches.

The milk that Mum used to fetch from the farm in the 1940s was so fresh it would still be warm. But unpasteurised milk was causing many people to contract tuberculosis. And towards the end of the war, when I was around five or six, I fell victim and was hospitalised. It was frightening because a lot of people died from tuberculosis in those days. I was one of the fortunate ones who made a full recovery, but not without the souvenir scar I have carried on my neck ever since, from where I had a TB abscess. The silver lining was my school naming me 'May Queen' to celebrate my return to health.

Unfortunately, not everyone was so lucky. One of Dennis' girlfriends got tuberculosis and without treatment, which simply wasn't available back then, she died like many others.

The End of the War

I may not remember what I did last week, but I remember the fireworks at the end of the war as plain as day. There were so many that Mum's hair caught fire!

I was celebrating at the front of the crowds on Llandudno Promenade when my mum said, 'If you touch one of those sailors' collars, it's good luck.' So, she picked me up and all the sailors kissed me, letting me touch their collars.

There were a lot of American GIs there celebrating, and I remember Auntie Emmie telling me to go and ask them for chewing gum. I was only little, but I went up to the sailors and was told to ask, 'Have you got any gum, chum?' She was such a cheeky monkey!

Overall, it was a very special, memorable day.

Auntie Emmie's sister, Auntie Gladys, also lived in Llandudno and she married one of the American GIs. Sadly, he never came back once he left after the war. She remained faithful to him forever and never remarried, hoping and believing he would come back, but he never did.

At the end of the war, there were trestle tables all the way along our avenue, filled with trifles, cakes, and other delights as we eagerly waited to celebrate our dads, husbands, brothers, and friends coming home. Some men hadn't been home since the very start of the war, so it was a momentous moment for us all.

One of my friends, Silvia, hadn't seen her dad one time throughout the war. She had only been a baby when he left. He had no idea what his daughter looked like, and when he walked down the road in his uniform, he turned to me and said, 'Are you Silvia? Are you my little girl?' I pointed out Silvia to him.

Dad stayed on for several months for the clean-up operation, so it was a long war for him. I remember how excited I was the day he came home. I can see him now, coming down the shared entry next to our house, wearing his 'demob' suit and holding a round sack containing all his clothes. The image of him at that moment will be ingrained in my memory forever. Mum and I made so much fuss around him that day.

We were so proud of him, and I loved listening to him recounting his war stories, just as Deborah did in later years.

Among his many stories, my dad often recounted the time he guarded Rudolf Hess, Hitler's right-hand man. Hess had flown a plane into Scotland hoping to negotiate peace with the UK, hoping he would be spared if he gave himself up. My dad was one of a handful of people chosen to escort Hess to where he would be held whilst awaiting trial. On one occasion, when my father was on guard duty, one of the German soldiers had been pining for a cigarette, and my dad gave him one. In return, he gave Dad a silver propelling pencil, which I still have in my tin!

Auntie Emmie's husband, Uncle Tom, also made it home safely, although he had a very difficult war and saw a lot of action. He also marched into Germany after the war with the British Army, which was rife with looting and disorder at the time. While there, Uncle Tom acquired a big clock with a pendulum that he was determined to bring home, so he marched across Germany with it under his arm! It was situated above the kitchen table throughout their lives.

The Start of a New Era

A fter the war, we went back to Stoke-on-Trent to our home on 21 Copes Avenue, now Churchfield Avenue, which was by a beautiful park called the Queen's Park in Dresden.

My dad went straight back to working at C H Smiths timber yard, and my mum went to work in the pottery industry. She was a lithographer, putting patterns on cups, saucers, and other pottery. However, although Mum worked, she was mainly at home looking after the family because Dad believed the place for a woman was in the home. She didn't mind, though, as she was very happy and she loved to cook, being naturally homely and maternal.

We built a lovely new life in that home, filled with wonderful memories with my parents.

We may not have had much, but we were inventive with what we had, and we never wasted or threw anything away. We often spent our Friday nights cutting up the local newspaper to use as toilet paper – probably the Evening Sentinel – threading it through a string and hanging it in the toilet. We never bought a toilet roll (I'm sure other people in my generation joined me in laughing when everyone panicked about loo roll during the early days of the pandemic!). We even pegged our own 'rag rugs', as we were never able to buy one. We cut up old materials, whether from an old coat or dress, before using a little tool like a hook to weave it into the rug. One time, when I was cutting some of the material, I didn't see the cat hiding underneath and I cut its ear off. It was a one-eared cat after that!

I will never forget Friday nights when I ran to meet Dad as he walked across the pit banks on his way home. His wages had been paid by then and he always had a shiny sixpence to give me as pocket money, which I carefully placed in the pocket of my little apron.

I fondly remember Dad's numerous rabbits that he enjoyed breeding to sell or give away. At one point, we had thirty-six! Dad even took pity on a local family living in poverty and gave them rabbits to keep as pets. However, shockingly, it transpired the family was cooking the rabbits for dinner! Dad would never have given them away with that intention.

It was wonderful to be able to experience holidays again, and I enjoyed going back to Llandudno. As a special treat, we also went to Blackpool to stay in a boarding house during Wakes Week, typically during the first week of August.

Following the war, it took time for people to redo their gardens, and not everyone got rid of their bomb shelters immediately. We had ours for quite a while and one of our neighbours even used theirs as a garden shed for many years. Deborah remembers playing in an old shelter, despite the fact she was born fifteen years after the war ended!

Grandad Owen used to enjoy working on my mother's garden, and this is where my lifelong love of gardening was born. He taught me how to grow plants, vegetables, and flowers, and he allocated me a square patch so that I could tend to my own little garden. He even put a sign next to it saying, 'Pauline's Garden'. He was such a lovely grandad.

Not everything was rosy after the war. We still had rations until around 1955 for one thing, and so many people lived in poverty.

In later years, I remember Ted telling me about how after the war, when his mum wanted to treat one of her five children to the cinema, she couldn't afford to take them all. She would take only one at a time, taking a bottle of medicine with her to pretend they had gone to the doctor. In Ted's house, the trips to the cinema were done in secrecy from the other kids, with the one child that was lucky enough to go sworn to secrecy.

People also got sick from working in treacherous jobs, with poor health and safety.

Grandma Jenkins, who worked in the pottery industry in Stoke-on-Trent, sadly got silicosis from the dust. So many people died of that in this area, my auntie included. At the same time, Grandad Jenkins got pneumoconiosis (a chest condition that many miners died from) as he worked in the coal mines, or the 'the pit' as they were known. The coal cut the lungs, the same way silicosis did from the pottery dust. People used to die of these conditions all the time sadly, despite the countryside chest hospitals, like Loggerheads near us, that attempted to allow people to breathe the cleaner air there.

My grandparents both died aged sixty, within six weeks of each other. I was only eight years old and it was extremely sad. One of the most heart-breaking things is that Grandma never even drew her first pension despite how hard she had worked for it. We still have her pension book saved in an envelope. It had arrived just days before she died.

By the time Grandma Jenkins died, Dennis was already living with us, so I was with him all the time. I loved him but he could be a nuisance sometimes, as I guess brothers can be. Once, he locked me in a cowshed on a nearby farm and it was a wonder I wasn't trampled to death by the huge number of cows in there with me! He thought it was a good laugh. Despite mischief like that, we remained very close throughout our lives.

The Smiths

❦

T his book can't go without a mention of the Smiths. The
owner of C H Smiths timber yard had a son, Hubert,
who was the same age as my dad, and they were good friends.
Hubert and his wife became my godparents, and we were so
close that I called them Uncle Hubert and Auntie Winnie.
There has never been a time that they weren't around. They
were so good to my family, and recently my daughter found a
receipt that exemplifies their kindness. The receipt shows that
the Smiths paid for my mum to have me in hospital rather than
at home, after already losing one baby. There was no NHS until
1948, so this would have been a huge help. They were lovely
people and my parents were best friends with them until the day
they died.

I have many childhood memories with the Smiths. Among
them, I remember the Smiths driving us around in their Jaguar,
and I loved staying with them at weekends. Their home was

luxurious compared to how we lived, with the treat of a bath ready every night before I went to bed! Most people just didn't have the means for daily baths back then. Likewise, you didn't have a change of clothes for every day. People used to say, 'You change your knickers every day, your dress once a week.'

In later years, the Smiths, after selling their timber yard, built a marvellous house in Dartmouth, in the South Devon area, which we often visited.

C H Smiths timber yard was sold to a big company, Tarmac, which went on to become Phoenix Timber, now called Phoenix Business Park.

Coincidentally, in later years Deborah's husband, my son-in-law Ray, had his first job working at C H Smiths timber yard.

Big Mo and Little Po: Special Friends

As a young girl, I had some very close friends: the two Sharman sisters, Joan and Muriel; Doreen Roberts; and Sylvia Tunstall, who lived across the road.

I was blessed with many wonderful cousins, too. On Mum's side, I had Uncle Bill's two sons, Arnold and Roy; and Uncle Sam's children, Bob and Cheryl. On Dad's side, I had Joyce, John, Barry, Maureen, Alan, Barbara, and Graham. I loved them all so much.

Maureen, my Auntie Polly's daughter, who was six months older than me, became a very close friend throughout my life, later becoming Deborah's godmother.

Maureen and I were always together. As I was smaller than her and quite dainty, they called us Big Mo and Little Po and you will see that illustrated in my wedding photos, where she was a bridesmaid, and is taller than me.

My School Years

Being devoted to her faith, my mother always made sure I went to Sunday school and in my early teenage years, I went to the evening church service as well. I was also a girl guide for many years.

The first school I attended was Dresden Infant and Junior School. I enjoyed the craft classes in junior school, but I struggled with maths and English.

As I didn't pass the 11-Plus exams, I went to Queensbury Secondary School. However, I was in the top group there, so I was clever in that school. Maureen, on the other hand, was very clever and she went to grammar school, having passed her 11-Plus exams.

Despite our separate schools, Maureen and I were always close friends.

At secondary school, between the ages of eleven to fifteen, I learned about practical things such as child welfare and cleaning. Practically, I learned how to be a housewife; to cook, iron, and look after a baby. I still have the book somewhere with all the instructions on what to do with a baby. It was just part of the curriculum.

I also had French lessons and two pen pals in France who I wrote to for several years. It has often been a wish of mine to find where they live now and reconnect.

A particularly memorable moment from my school days was the Queen's Coronation held on 2 June 1953, when there were a lot of events planned around the country. It was a wonderful time.

In the lead up to the coronation, it had been promised that the Queen was going to visit Stoke-on-Trent. In anticipation of her visit, new tarmac was laid on Copes Avenue, where we lived, and trees were planted along Chaplin Road. Copes Avenue was even renamed Churchfield Avenue. Disappointingly, her visit was called off at the last minute. At least our road had been done!

To mark her coronation, my whole class went on a school trip to London where we had a bus tour around the city. Unfortunately for me, I suffer from travel sickness, so I was being sick all the time. Still, it was interesting to see all the decorations and lights, the soldiers, Buckingham Palace's guards, and all the preparations underway for the planned events.

Teenage Years

When I left school at fifteen, Mum wanted me to work in a dress shop called Hoppers, a posh ladies' and children's wear shop, which also had a men's department. She was so proud of me when I got the job. Part of my role was to dress the window upstairs with coats, dresses, and jumpers, which was good fun. While there, I also used to go shopping with Mr Hopper's mother, at Mr Hopper's request, because she needed a companion and somebody to carry her bags. That was an experience in itself! I had a lot of fun working there, and the experience reminds me of the show, 'Are You Being Served?'

During that time, being a teenager, it was exciting to be able to save up for clothes and sometimes I made new pieces from fabric or old clothes that had been thrown out by somebody else. I loved clothes and always wanted new outfits.

My best friend at Hoppers was Joan Rhodes, and we are still close friends to this day. At work, we had to call each other 'Miss Rhodes' and 'Miss Owen'. We used to do everything together and had so much fun as teenagers, often going to Longton Town Hall together to dance. Joan even came with me to Llandudno sometimes, to stay with Auntie Emmie, which was great fun.

Meeting Ted

B y the time I was sixteen, I had encountered a few casual romances, but none had been serious. Although, one of these boys deserves a mention, as I turned him down when he asked me out, and then he went on to become a very famous actor!

One day, aged sixteen, I went to Dresden youth club to play my records, which was always fun. That day, I met a boy called Ted – short for Edward – who was also a member there. Little did I know he would play such a huge part in my life, becoming my future husband.

Ted recalled that I had a clipboard when he met me, as I had been trying to rally people to come to Blackpool on a youth club trip. When I asked if he wanted to go, he put his name on the list. A little later I walked over to him and said, 'It looks like it's just me and you.' The rest is history.

The first thing he did was walk me back from the youth club, but only after frightening me... It was dark and I was walking through Dresden Churchyard with a friend of mine when all of a sudden, Ted jumped out from behind a headstone, taking me by surprise! In the process of doing this, he managed to rip the seat off his trousers against a tree trunk! It might be funny to look back at this now, but at the time I was a nervous wreck! Mum was livid when she found out, telling me that I should never speak to him again. So, he made a bad first impression, but he made up for it and would go on to become my loving husband.

In the days following Ted's surprise in the graveyard, I learnt that I already knew his twin sister, Kathy, from piano lessons I had with her. I hasten to add that I passed all my piano exams to get the teaching qualifications! Through talking to Kathy, I learnt more about Ted, which brought us closer and I became very interested in him. Looking back, I think I liked him from the very first time we met. But it wasn't until we went to his cousin's bonfire that we had our first date (if you can call it a date). It was certainly a special moment for us, and we took some fireworks to set them off.

Writing about the night of the bonfire is really taking me back.

As Ted lived in the avenue above me, on Fairfield Avenue, it was easy to see each other often, and we never had a chaperone. He was a gentleman, always walking me home and often treating me to special things. Ted spoiled me; he couldn't take me to the pictures without buying me a box of chocolates and he bought me beautiful jewellery, too. In fact, throughout our lives, he always got me the most beautiful presents. On my eighteenth birthday, he bought me a beautiful gold watch (that I still have today) and his mum turned to him and said, 'What have you bought her that for? You should have bought her an engagement ring, not a watch!' Although we had been together for two years by that point, there wasn't a rush to get engaged, and I didn't mind.

At first, my parents were unsure of Ted and our relationship as they had wanted me to marry someone from their church. Ted's family were Catholic, you see, which was frowned upon by people in my church back then. But my parents came to accept him over time, and it turned out that he was more a son to them than anyone could have been. They really did love him.

Ted had a big, loud, fun family, in contrast to my very quiet, calm family where no one ever exchanged a cross word. As one of five, he had an older brother Jack, married to Margaret, two older sisters, Peggy and Doreen, married to Derek and George, and his twin, Kathy, married to Tony.

His family were entertaining to be around, talking over each other incessantly. When I first went to meet them, I couldn't believe it. Everybody was talking at the same time, and I just sat there, thinking, 'Oh gosh, what's going on here?'

Ted's siblings were lovely though, and they have given me nephews and nieces who I adore!

When Ted first came over to my house for tea on a Sunday, in 1956, there was a rather unfortunate event. In those days you had a kitchen as well as a scullery, where you had your sink and cooker. In our scullery, my mother kept a kettle on a little window that was very high up. Kettles didn't switch off automatically back then, you had to turn them off manually. That day, while it was boiling, it fell and spilt all over me, giving me a terrible burn that scarred me for life. Ted was scared and upset but took me to the hospital immediately, where I stayed for a long time. It was the first time that Ted had been to my house, and he would have been nervous, so you can imagine how horrible it was for such a special occasion to end that way, poor thing.

While I was in the hospital, Ted bought me an Elvis LP, while Elvis was still a new phenomenon. It was an early album that came with a book of photographs of Elvis, too. He also bought me a red Dansette record player, which was very precious to me. Over the years, it passed down to Deborah, who had it on a unit we had made for her in her bedroom.

Elvis soon became a sensation and his music was constantly played in youth clubs and cafés. I loved his music, as did Ted, and I never steered away from choosing Heartbreak Hotel on the jukebox. Elvis was so different to the likes of Pat Boone, Frank Sinatra, Dean Martin, and other popular musicians in the 1950s who wrote love song ballads. With Elvis came rock and roll; his songs were upbeat music and created so much fun. Dancing was soon transformed to the bop, which Ted and I loved!

In later years we were dancing every week and we went to dance classes, too. We loved the Latin American dances and more, and it was something we enjoyed throughout our lives together, but I will write about that later in this book.

PAULINE HAND

Petrol Pumps and Pottery

While I was courting Ted, I changed jobs in order to earn more money. I was earning a meagre two pounds and eleven shillings a week and working until six o'clock on a Saturday, which was a nuisance because I had to go home to get dressed before going to the town hall to dance. Eager not to miss out, I used to queue up with my rollers in!

Doreen, Ted's older sister, helped find me a better-paid job working at the local petrol station, where she worked for a man called Mr Reeder. There, I served petrol and washed cars, windscreens, and checked tyre pressures. I often offered to help with smaller odd jobs, too, so that customers left me a tip or told me to keep the change. Towards the end of my shift, at ten o'clock in the evening, I had to take the huge, frightening Alsatian guard dog for a walk around the block. Finally, I locked up all the petrol pumps and counted the day's takings before walking home up Blurton Road and Drubery Lane. That job didn't last too long, though, and both Doreen and I had to find other work.

After this, I went to work in the pottery industry, which is what my mum had dreaded all along given what had happened to Grandma. She always said, 'You're not going work on a pot bank.' But I did.

Initially, my job involved helping a man who was putting big trays of pots in the boiling hot kilns. That made for hard work. I didn't enjoy it and was exasperated by my boss who was a horrible little man. Eventually, I was allowed to learn slide lithography; the method of transferring designs and patterns onto cups by wetting the patterns in big troughs. I preferred doing that for a while. I also did gilding, which was interesting, although getting gold on my apron by mistake meant taking it off and burning it to take the gold off!

When I was about eighteen, the companies in the area held a Miss Staffordshire Pottery beauty contest. When picking somebody to represent our factory, I was selected. I agreed to do it, but only if I could make my dress because I didn't want to buy one. With the money provided, I bought kingfisher blue satin fabric and made a dress with netting underneath it to make it stick out. With the leftover money, I bought some perfume and makeup. At the contest, although it was fun, I remained true to myself. Some of the girls were a bit saucy with the judges, showing off their legs and such. Also, I couldn't help but notice that girls from big-named companies like Beswick, Wedgewood, and Dolton had a much better chance. I didn't win but it was fun, and Ted happily clapped in support when I went onto the stage.

Wedding Bells

Ted and I were having so much fun courting that it was only natural for my gold watch to be trumped by an engagement ring, decisively progressing to the next stage of our relationship.

In 1958, Ted and I went to look at engagement rings in a jewellery shop in Hanley. Before we got married, he was earning very well through his job contracting at Florence Colliery, so he bought me the most exquisite ring. It was very plain, with three lovely diamonds fitted in a row, signifying 'I Love You'.

Instead of a big engagement party, I worked hard to save for my 'bottom drawer' – I was always saving for my bottom drawer! In those days, it was normal to get engaged and then save for household items such as linen and crockery. I was constantly adding to mine, helped by Mum taking me once a week to a shop up in the high street where she would buy me a present. That shop had the most beautiful, expensive saucepans, which I still have today.

By the time I got married, I had a laundry basket, pegs, and many other household items. I still use these things to this day, as well as some of our wedding presents, because they have enormous sentimental value. Everything had significance then, everything was needed. Nowadays, if you need something you just put it in your trolley at the supermarket and that's it.

To buy my wedding dress, I went with my mum to Worrall's in Longton, by the fire station. I chose a ballerina dress that hung just below the knee. Short dresses were only just coming into fashion, so much so that people getting married a few weeks before me wouldn't even have tried a dress such as the one I chose! It was white with rosebud details down the front, with layers and layers of petticoat sticking out like a ballerina's tutu. It was beautiful, like the dresses you see on Strictly Come Dancing. Even though it was expensive – the petty coat itself costing me four guineas, which was a lot of money – both Mum and I loved it and the decision was made. Deborah made use of it, too, later down the line, when she dressed up in it as a little girl, spinning around the living room when 'Come Dancing' was on TV.

Choosing a church to marry in wasn't simple because my church, which I still go to now, was the Elim church. Whereas Ted's family went to a Catholic church. So, we compromised on neutral ground and got married in Dresden Church of England. It was a bit of a shock to Ted's family that we weren't getting married in the Catholic church, but the solution felt right for us.

On 11 June 1960, aged twenty, Ted and I got married. I had a lovely wedding and truly felt like my parent's princess. Mum was constantly there when I was getting ready; dressing me, seeing to me, helping me with my hair, arranging my headdress and veil, and making sure everything was alright. The manageress of Hoppers came up to my bedroom to see me getting dressed, too. It was such fun.

My cousin Maureen was my maid of honour, and Ted's youngest cousins, Christine and Jennifer, were bridesmaids. My best friend Joan was there, too, but in those days you weren't allowed to be a bridesmaid if you were married. Ted's best man was his older brother by ten years, Jack. He was the obvious choice because they worked together, drank together, and Jack looked after Ted. They were the epitome of best friends and it was special to have our nearest and dearest by our side on such a special day.

Down the aisle, I carried a Bible rather than a bouquet, with a ribbon that trailed down with dark red roses. I kept those roses and pressed them in a book, which I should still have somewhere.

When I got to the top of the aisle, Ted just looked at me, admiring how lovely I looked in my dress.

It was a lovely service, led by Father Paton Jones who was very well known in the area, and who latterly christened Deborah.

At one point, Mum was rearranging the bridesmaid's dresses for the photographs when a huge gust of wind came and blew her dress over her head! The photographer somehow captured the moment, with all the ladies holding on to their hats.

We had around one hundred people at our wedding reception in an upstairs room at the Dunrobin Hotel, which was quite a lot of people to invite in those days! All the family came from Derby, Gloucester, and local areas, too. We liked the Dunrobin, which had a lovely space as it was a huge pub in which Ted used to go for a drink. In the evening, there was dancing and a buffet. Traditionally, in those days, the bride and groom didn't stay for the dancing, and it was time for us to head off on our honeymoon. So, after I changed into a beautiful royal blue suit with a blue cape collar, and a white, raffia straw pillbox hat, we left for Blackpool on our honeymoon. I thought I looked wonderful. I truly felt like a famous actress, with all those people cheering and waving us off.

A Honeymoon in Blackpool

❧

The details of our honeymoon can't be told without explaining the car we were driving in.

Even though Ted's mum and dad couldn't drive, his mum had decided to buy a car for their five children to use. Almost all cars were black in 1959. To put that into context, one of Henry Ford's most famous mottos was, 'You can have any colour you want as long as it's black!'

When Ted's mum went to look at the car, she was about to buy a black Ford Zodiac, but Ted turned up at the garage and saw the first coloured car! It was yellow and white, and no one had seen anything like it. He turned to his mum and said, 'Have that one!' And that she did.

And that is the short tale of how we came to have such a fabulous car for our honeymoon.

My friends had stuck tin cans and streamers onto the car so that after our wedding, we departed with all the tin cans and that noise behind us. My sister-in-law, Doreen, wasn't impressed, as that car was used by all their family, and I can remember her saying, 'Be careful you don't put your sticky plasters on the car!' We removed the cans and streamers a little further down the road.

When we arrived in Blackpool there were constant crowds of people eager to get a closer look at our unusual car. It was such fun.

Ted took a week off for our honeymoon and we had a lovely time despite the mixed weather. Thankfully, Ted had been there before with his friends, so he knew his way around. We stayed at the Red Court Hotel, went to the fair, to the beach, and went shopping, even though we didn't have an awful lot of money to spend. But, as we were trying to create a home together, we bought little things for the house.

Further down the line, Ted bought that car off his mum and we owned it for many years. Eventually, he sold it to a local taxi firm that used it as a novelty car for special occasions, and latterly it was showcased in classic car shows.

Roxburghe Avenue

In the post-war days, people didn't have much money.
Families had to look after each other, and if one person had
something it was shared. If you wanted to buy something, you
saved. Therefore, it was very unusual to have a house to go to as
young newlyweds. Even honeymoons were unusual. More
commonly, people moved in with their parents after their
weddings and lived in their front room or similar.

Ted had started as an apprentice blacksmith at the mine, but
then he went underground with his dad and brother, Jack. It
was a tough job, but as he was contracting, he was earning good
money. He managed to accumulate savings that gave us an
amazing start to our married life.

We came across a house we liked on Roxburghe Avenue and my
Uncle Hubert advised on work that might need doing to it. His
advice was helpful, as we were young and inexperienced, needing
to know if it was worth buying. Also, as Uncle Hubert owned C

H Smiths timber yard, he knew builders that were trustworthy and could advise us.

We were able to buy that lovely house thanks to Ted's high income. For context, you could buy a terraced house in Stoke-on-Trent for £50 at the time, but we had a £500 deposit, so we bought that semi-detached house for £2,500. It wasn't heard of at that time. People couldn't believe it because we were only young. Ted even had to prove that he had the deposit! But, for all the luck we had, Ted had earned the money from a tough job.

Dad helped a lot with doing the DIY for our first home, ensuring it was all done up and nicely decorated, with fresh curtains and fitted wardrobes in all three bedrooms. Ted would spend time with my dad, watching him and learning as Dad was brilliant with all these things. That is where Ted got his love of DIY from. Working together, they went as far as knocking rooms through, putting French doors and windows in (which were modern at the time), and Ted built a lovely stone fireplace in the living room.

On entering the house there was a big hallway, with a living room and dining room to the right and a kitchen straight at the end. The stairs led from the hall to a landing serving three bedrooms and a family bathroom. Then, the sunken garden was accessed down a few steps off the back of the house. That garden was so beautiful. All around the edge were two pear trees, four apple trees, damson bushes, lovely flowers, and various shrubs with blackcurrants, strawberries, blackberries, gooseberries, and redcurrants. Consequently, I was always making jams and never had to buy any. My damson jam tasted nothing like the one you can buy, as mine had two pounds of sugar in it and was far sweeter! As we had more fruit than we could eat, I made all sorts of pies. Later down the line, when I got a freezer, I even froze my bean crop to eat throughout the year.

The house was close to where we both lived as children, on Churchfield Avenue. Next door to us lived Mrs Stanway, the headmistress of the Dresden school where I used to go, and, interestingly, she was still headmistress when Deborah went there. It was a little scary living next to my old headmistress, even though we got on well!

Almost everyone on the close was elderly and posh, so there were lessons to take heed of when we first moved in. I had just come back from my honeymoon on a Saturday when I thought it was a great day to hang the washing in the garden on Sunday, with the sun shining. I was quickly put in my place by a neighbour who said, 'We don't do that here on a Sunday!' To this day, I will not hang my washing on a Sunday.

Soon after our marriage, Ted's work contract came to an end, his job changed, and he went on to a much smaller wage. It was a bit of a shock as, all of a sudden, we had a huge mortgage to pay on a smaller income. Looking back, paying the mortgage became a real driver for us, knowing money was scarce.

We cut back as much as possible. I remember only being able to afford a quarter of ham to put on Ted's sandwich, but none for myself. That period was very tough, but it was the same for everyone around us. So, we didn't realise it so much, as there was nothing better to compare it to, and no great expectations. Things are so plentiful now that I look back and think, 'Crikey, how did I manage?'

The Pitter-Patter of Baby Feet

Throughout our marriage, we were blessed with support from our parents, relatives, and friends, who were always lovely to us as a young couple. Auntie Dorothy and Uncle Lol (short for Lawrence Owen – Dad's cousin), who lived in a large house directly opposite the park, were among these people. I have used the wedding presents they gave me – a beautiful baking set – my whole married life.

On a trip to Cornwall a few months after our wedding, I was being sick every day and I soon realised I was expecting Deborah.

At the time, we were staying in a place called Caddy's Farm, where Ted's family used to go and have a lot of fun. Now, I certainly wasn't brought up to complain and I wasn't posh. But there were spiders and cobwebs everywhere which petrified me! It was not a good place to be, particularly when suffering from nausea and morning sickness. To make matters worse, I saw a ghost in that bedroom! I don't believe in the supernatural, and I find it hard to believe it happened, but I saw what looked like a Quaker man with a Quaker hat. Perhaps I was poorly and seeing things, but it felt very real at the time and it terrified me!

Despite the spiders, ghosts, and nausea, it was a lovely holiday, and we have a photograph showing the whole family together there. It was a special place for the Hand family as by chance, Harriet Hand, Ted's mum, had discovered their family originated from Cornwall. This is a story that deserves a mention!

Mrs Hand was reading the Catholic Herald one day when she read an article by a Dom at Downside Abbey and saw his last name was Trethowan. As her maiden name was Trathowen, a name that nobody seemed to share, she was curious to know if she was connected to the Trethowan family. She wrote to the Dom, and when his reply came, she was astounded. He explained that her name had indeed been misspelt. Mrs Hand confirmed what she had been told by looking at her father's birth certificate, which showed not only the correct spelling of the name as Trethowan, but also that he had been born in Constantine in Cornwall. Her family had indeed been calling themselves Trathowen, and still do that to this day. Not only did it transpire that Trethowan was a family name originating from Constantine, but it turned out to be a rare name, meaning that every person bearing that name was related across the world. A one-family name. Ted's mum was very proud of the family name after that, and we went to Cornwall for all our holidays together, curiously looking around the churchyards to find Ted's ancestors.

Back home after some wonderful Cornish air, we were a bit shy about telling our mothers that I was expecting a baby, and I remember turning to Ted and saying, 'You tell my mother, and then tell your mother that we're having this baby.'

He did tell them, and I still remember him saying, 'Pauline is in the family way.' Yes, that was something people used to say!

My pregnancy progressed without major issues and my mother kindly accompanied me to the hospital for my prenatal appointments. In those days, husbands weren't as involved with those check-ups, and Ted wouldn't have been able to get out of work anyway.

Deborah was born exactly ten months after we got married, on 11 April 1961, when I was twenty-one years old.

She was born in a hospital, which was unusual, as in the 1960s most babies were born at home. My labour was very long and awful and the midwife had to use forceps to help our baby into this world. However, it was wonderful holding our new baby girl, Deborah. I felt so sorry for her though, as she was so fragile with an injured eye where the forceps had cut her. It was a mess and they stitched her up badly, leaving a scar to this day.

Deborah was a very good baby and we had a lovely time together. I used to go to the baby clinic once a week, probably on a Tuesday, with a lovely neighbour who was a friend of mine – sadly, this lady later died in a car accident, leaving her son, Deborah's school friend, with no choice but to go into care, which wasn't uncommon in those days when the mother died.

Something that makes me smile now is thinking back to Deborah as a baby, with her bald little head. I had lovely hair when I was little, so I had been expecting a baby with a lot of hair! But Deborah had no hair at all. Let it be known, she did eventually grow lovely, blonde, curly hair but there was no sign of it until she turned two.

For a while, I didn't go back to work when Deborah was born. My mother-in-law had offered to look after her, but I wanted to take care of her myself and enjoy being a mother to an extremely happy child who was always full of life.

I loved our simple outings, such as collecting Deborah from the nursery, when I would stop at the shop on the way home to buy her a 'lucky bag' filled with a surprise mix of sweets. Back at home, we watched our favourite television programmes like

'Watch with Mother', which included programmes like 'The Flowerpot Men' and 'Andy Pandy'. We both treasure these memories to this day.

Deborah recently told me how she remembers coming home from nursery or school on Mondays, the day I did all the washing and hung it to dry by the warm coal fire. On Mondays, I also cooked lobby, a typical Staffordshire casserole cooked with vegetables and leftover meats and gravy from our Sunday joints (you re-used whatever you had leftover in those days!).

It's sometimes the simple things that stand out, and I find it touching to think that the smell of lobby cooking, and laundry by the fire, bring Deborah back to her childhood and our home.

Although Deborah was an only child, there were always plenty of children to play with at my parent's home on Churchfield Avenue, as well as her many cousins congregating at Ted's parent's home. She had so many friends and cousins that we always had to have two birthday parties for her; in fact, it seemed as if there was a birthday party for someone at any given time! Each year, Deborah's first party was for the family, with all her first cousins; Andrew and Gail, John and Gregory, Mark and Catherine, Victoria and Daniel. The following Saturday we had another party with her friends from school. On such special occasions, we dressed Deborah in beautiful outfits I had made, and she always looked so beautiful. We put on delicious spreads of party foods like jelly and ice creams and organised party games such as pass the parcels or musical chairs, which were such fun.

Come Christmas, we were always having to find different hiding places for Deborah's presents, either under a bed or in our loft. It was a slick operation; I would wait until Deborah had gone to bed, hastily wrap the presents with nice Christmas paper, and hide the pile of presents at the bottom of the bed, covered by a sheet. As she grew older and wiser, Deborah spotted them – they weren't hidden well enough!

'Has Father Christmas been?' She would ask, excitedly.

'No, he hasn't.' We replied with a straight face, 'That's just a shadow you think you can see!'

We loved Christmas and shared such special times.

In the morning, with the unwrapping of presents completed, we went to Ted's mother's house, as we passed hers on the way to my mum's. Mrs Hand never failed to have a drink of Drambuie ready for us. I didn't drink much but not wanting to come across rudely, I drank it. It was like drinking a medicine; even if you don't like it, you have got to do it! We then went to Mum's for traditional dinner and tea. And I know Deborah will tell you some more about our Christmas experiences in her chapter.

I can't go without mentioning our budgies, too! We never had pets, as Ted didn't want them in the house, so Deborah didn't get the same experience as me. I grew up with cats and a dog (my dearest Skippy!). Nonetheless, we always had a budgie and it was always, without fail, called Toby: Toby I, Toby II, and Toby III.

A Hard-Working Life

I n the early years of our marriage, we lived day by day, working hard to pay the mortgage. Luxuries weren't an option. For instance, our car was only insured part of the year, leaving us on foot most of the time. We lived near our work, but it was still a nuisance at times.

Taking care of the house took a lot of work back then. Most household machines and commodities were slower or inexistent. My washing machine was large and took a lot of effort; after filling it with water from the kitchen tap, it would beat your washing, spinning it round and round. At the end of the washing cycle, you would pull your clothes through a mangle. I never had a twin tub, which was the following step for most people, as I got an automatic machine next instead (and what a revelation that was!). Modern technology has made household chores so much easier.

Fridges were a rarity, too, and we had a larder instead that lived under the stairs with tiled walls. There, I would set jelly and store covered meats and tinned foods. Saying this, the little bedroom upstairs was so cold in the winter it was as good as a larder! We didn't have central heating, and our storage heaters – as modern looking as they were – didn't stretch to keeping the house warm day and night. As the first heating system, filled with bricks, they would heat up overnight, when the cost of electricity was cheapest, and then release their warmth through the day.

During this period in our lives, our local friends and neighbours were an important friendship group for us. We would take the babies around the park, spending our days together catching up when we weren't working or doing house chores.

Mick and Val, who were good friends of ours, often came to visit. We spent a lot of time together. Val was only around twenty, and I was around twenty-one, and we could be a bit daft and silly together. Once, Val came over and was having such a good time with Deborah as a baby on the rocking chair, singing lullabies, that she tipped it straight back! Ted and I would often go to Florence Club with Mick and Val, dancing into the night, sometimes even four times a week! They were good friends that Deborah grew up calling Auntie Val and Uncle Mick.

We then had Mick and Wendy, our next door neighbours, and Val and Graham, who lived a few doors away. They were all wonderful friends.

As Val didn't have her son until a few years later, she used to make such a fuss over Deborah. Val and Graham were one of the only people we knew who had a fridge. Deborah loved going there to make a lolly in a cup in their icebox, with orange juice and a stick. She was spoilt by our friends!

Darker Days

〇〜〇

S adly, the early years of our marriage saw some darker days.

In 1962, after having had Deborah, I learnt that I was expecting another child but soon after he was born, on 17 January 1963, we learnt that he wouldn't survive more than a few hours. I was absolutely distraught, and I still suffer from that grief now.

It was extremely difficult to process, but I insisted on seeing my little boy. He was so different from Deborah, with lots of dark hair, like Ted. We named him Edward, after Ted, and we had him christened in the hospital. He was buried in Longton cemetery.

The second baby I lost was born on 31 October 1964. We had intended to call him Martin, but as he was a stillbirth, we weren't even able to get him a birth certificate and I was told he was incinerated at the hospital.

At one point, I considered adoption, especially as when we lost our second baby the hospital informed us that we could go to the top of the adoption list. However, Ted didn't feel he could bring up someone else's child. And, as he was the man of the house – the decision-maker – I never argued against him. We never adopted.

In the lead up to both pregnancies, I remember having a basket full of baby clothes I had knitted, but neither baby ever made it home. The local coalman's wife was having a baby around that time, so my mum gave him all the baby things before I returned from the hospital, to save me further upset.

It was a difficult period and I was living with constant sadness. It meant I couldn't fully enjoy the first five years of Deborah's life. Deborah, therefore, spent a lot of the time with my mother who thought the world of her and cared for her lovingly.

My grief wasn't helped by some people often saying, 'This is Pauline, she's only got one child.' I felt as though my name had almost become that sentence because it was said so much.

With no siblings of my own, I didn't really have anyone to talk to about what I was experiencing at the time. And I didn't want to discuss anything with my mother, as it was difficult for her, too. I held the grief inside for a long time, but I do talk about it now.

As if things weren't difficult enough, in 1965 Uncle Dennis had a near-fatal car accident that left him with life-changing spinal injuries. He couldn't walk and was in a bad state. Mum had to look after him, so she gave up her job. He lived with her until he was sixty when he married Muriel.

Because of all that sadness, I didn't go to church for almost twenty years. It wasn't until the 1980s that I started going back when I was inspired by Deborah, who got involved with a youth group at the Elim Church when she was sixteen. Nonetheless, my faith guided me through that dark period. As a Christian, I knew that the Everlasting Arms are underneath you, and round about you, so you will never hit rock bottom. Remembering that is very important to me.

Ted's 'tough love' was also helpful through my darker days. He was the strict one in the family and often said, 'Pull yourself together Pauline.' It makes me smile remembering him saying that, as it really worked with me. In fact, the words 'pull yourself together' have become somewhat of a motto in my life, and now they have passed down the generations, too. When Ted died, which I will write about later, it was Deborah's turn to remind me to pull myself together and it really helped. She would say, 'Come on Mum, pull yourself together.'

In the 1960s, though, when I lost the two babies, as much as I tried to pull myself together, the depression overwhelmed me. Losing a child is the worst death of all. The grief tested me in every way I could imagine, and I did have to take medication to help me through.

For anybody going through similar grief now, I would say to them to just keep relying on their faith and to remember that things happen for a reason. I don't know what that reason is – don't ask me – but things do happen for a reason. Also, although it can be good to talk about things, it's not *always* good to have things out in the open, it can be habit-forming talking about them all the time. Ultimately, life goes on.

Onwards and Upwards

A fter my second stillbirth, my doctor suggested I returned to work to distract myself. In those days, children didn't really go to nursery, which meant seeking special dispensation on the basis of my depression to find Deborah a place. Deborah was only two when she went to Westfield Nursery in Lockets Lane.

It definitely helped me to have a life away from home. I began working as a cleaner at Longton Cottage Hospital, but not for long because I was always coming home with sore throats and passing them to Deborah.

One day, as I was leafing through the local paper to look at the job advertisements, I saw an advert for a job at the market. The prospect of working at a fruit stall, with all the comings and goings of people, sounded interesting and I applied.

The next thing I knew, the Derbyshires, the owners of the fruit stall, came to our house! I was sunbathing on our back lawn, having been a sun worshipper all my life, when the doorbell rang. I answered the door in my bikini (and I was known for my flashy bikinis!). It was quite the surprise when I found myself face-to-face with the people who introduced themselves as Jack and Arthur Derbyshire, the owners of the fruit stall that I had applied to work at. It transpired they had come to check I was trustworthy, given that the job meant handling a lot of cash. I was thrilled to be offered the job, and it was the start of a great friendship with the Derbyshires who I would grow to love like family.

My shifts were on Wednesdays, Fridays, and Saturdays. Ted always met me at the end of my shifts when he was able to, so we could go home together. When I wasn't working at the fruit stall, I was working on the garden or cleaning our house. The new routine was good for me, as were the friends I made through work, and things started to look brighter. The depression eased, and I just loved meeting the people at the market, getting to know them as they returned every week for their fruit.

The Derbyshire's fruit stall was very much a family business. I worked alongside Jack and Arthur and got to know them extremely well. Forgive my memory, but either Jack or Arthur had twins, John and Michael, who also worked on the stall, as did another of their sons, also called Arthur! Les, Jack and Arthur's nephew (who we coincidentally live by now!), also worked on the stall, as did Josie, one of their wives, and another lady called Winnie. Their fruit stall, which is still in Longton Market today, was massive!

Even now, when we go there, you can sense the love shared between the Derbyshires and me. They have known me for a long time, after all. I remember the young boys coming round to deliver the fruit and vegetables to us on a Friday night, and I always gave them a treat. So, our families have been intertwined through the years, even after I stopped working there.

It wasn't all work during this period, of course. On some Saturday nights, Ted and Deborah collected me straight from work to drive all the way to Llandudno. We arrived at Auntie Emmie's house just in time for one of her famous Welsh lamb sandwiches, looking forward to enjoying her Sunday roast.

We also had joyous times going dancing and to concerts. In the early 1960s, Ted and I were on the front row of a Beatles concert in Llandudno. Despite the fact neither of us were big fans it was such a fun occasion. Of course, we would have preferred to see our favourites; the Rolling Stones, Shirley Bassey, and Tom Jones. Delilah is still one of my favourite songs! But the Beatles were very good live, though Ted was a bit overwhelmed by the women on the front row screaming in excitement.

The day after this concert, when Ted and I were walking along the Llandudno Pier with Mum and Dad, I spotted the Beatles on the pier and said, 'Oh, look out! It's the Beatles!'

The next thing I knew my dad was looking on the floor for beetles!

In 1968 the Beatles were very famous. Kathy and Tony came to our house and invited Ted to go with the other men who were having their hair cut in the 'Beatle cut' style, a flat cut style, unlike the popular teddy boy style. Ted had to wear a cap for weeks because he had very thick and strong hair, so he had to retrain it to stay down.

Ted's Career

Ted started working in the Florence Colliery coal mine when he was just fifteen, and he persevered through his difficult job for eighteen years. The mine had three different shafts, and workers went up to a mile underground to reach whatever area they were working on. It wasn't a job for the faint-hearted.

Unlike his dad, Mr Hand, who had never known anything else and worked underground for a total of fifty-two years, Ted hated working in the pit and I believe the work was never suited to him. But knowing their dad wouldn't work anywhere else, Ted and Jack agreed to work there until their dad's retirement. The reason for sticking by their dad was simple: pit work was extremely dangerous, so teams were often made up of family members to increase their safety. Families were much more likely to look after each other, listening for any noises or creaks. Ted and Jack didn't want to leave their dad to work in a team with others. So, Ted loyally endured a long career in the pit until his dad finally retired.

As a family unit, they had their own crutting team; the team that cut through rock, getting rid of the stones, to get the coal.

Every day was worrying for me, staying at home and hoping that nothing would happen to Ted. Injuries and even deaths weren't uncommon.

For example, my mum's brother, Uncle Bill, had a terrible accident in the pit when he was fourteen. Fortunately, he recovered and lived a long life, but only after having a metal plate fixed onto his head. Another story that sticks out from Ted's working days is when Ted came home close to tears one day. I was horrified to hear that an accident had left a poor guy decapitated and Ted had helped bring his body out. That was a real turning point for Ted, and he never wanted to stay after that.

Even so, it was not always doom and gloom. Ted had a lot of experience with what was called 'packing down the pit'; neatly putting rocks to one side. It meant he could build a beautiful dry-stone wall! He was always bringing fossils home, too, most memorably a squashed, fossilized mouse head on a piece of coal.

Another fun memory is from when the mining company had some baths put in, so the workers didn't have to wash at home. Remember, they were covered in black by the end of the day! But Mrs Hand thought the idea of men bathing together was indecent, and so Mr Hand, Ted, and Jack never used them. Instead, they went to Jack's house, as it was the closest to the pit, and all three of them had their bath there every day. Everyone remembered them because of this. On the day of the opening of the baths, Ted's mum walked up to the Lord Mayor sharing her views on the matter, declaring, 'It's not happening in my family!'

They all came home laughing from that event.

Talking about baths has reminded me of when I was at Jack's house with his wife, Margaret when Ted, Jack, and Mr Hand returned from work for their bath. It was the first time I had seen Ted covered in black, head to toe. Three figures walked up the garden path towards the house and I had no idea who was who!

Ted was quite particular about not wanting the coal to stain the skin under his eyes as it looked like black eyeliner. To ensure this wouldn't happen, he smeared Vaseline around his eyes to get the black off at the end of the day.

As I always expected, the day Mr Hand retired Ted left his job too. There was no reason to stay. Jack, on the other hand, stayed on until he got a job on the bank, becoming the train driver that brought the coal from one place to the other.

I remember that day well. Ted came to me and said, 'Let's go shopping in Hanley.' There, we saw an advert for a job at a Michelin tyres factory and that is where he worked until he retired early at fifty-two.

He enjoyed working at the Michelin factory, thriving in the corporate environment. He loved his job and he made lots of friends there. After all those years in the pit, he found the work easy and pleasing, although he always worked hard. It was made all the more fun by his two brothers-in-law working there, too.

At this point, our lives began to change, and we were able to enjoy a few more luxuries. The car, for one, was insured year-round! Ted worked hard, taking few days off, unlike at the pit, when he tried to get by on a three-day working week to reduce his working hours there.

We suddenly felt very well off and things were looking up, especially when I began working full-time, too, and we got a new car – a Ford Capri. It was bright yellow and marvellous.

Supportive Grandparents

I worked at the Derbyshire's fruit stall until Deborah went to Sandon High School when she was twelve years old. She had been at Dresden Church of England Middle School before that, the same school I had been to.

Her first day in high school marked my first day at a company called Tootle Fashions, which was situated in Normacot. For those who may not have heard of Tootle, it was a brand of posh men's shirts, and the company is still going today. It was my job to help make these very expensive shirts and other clothes for men.

Hard as the work was in the sewing factory, my time there was made joyous by the good friends I made. The girls I worked alongside were mostly around ten years younger than me and always full of life, ready to share their funny stories. There was always something going on and I was entertained all the time. Even after work, I laughed until it hurt when trying to explain the stories to Ted and Deborah. One girl, Janet Hopkins, who I worked alongside in later jobs, too, was always full of tales and I knew she would brighten every day without fail. One of Janet's stories has stuck with me through the years; she told me how her family had a motorbike with a sidecar and one time, when she was in the sidecar, it got detached and sent her straight through a hedge! There were a million stories like that.

We always took the job seriously, ensuring all our work was done, but we found plenty of time for some innocent mischief, too. On one of these occasions, the girls placed me in one of the big wagons and wheeled me through the factory, laughing all the way. We also had Christmas parties with a fancy dress theme. Being good at sewing, we made all our outfits and always put together a funny costume for the boss, too, making him look really silly. The parties were always delightful.

As I worked full-time, mum organised Ted's lunch at her house. She always provided lovely, cooked meals for him before he left for work on the afternoon shift.

I was an only child and so Deborah was the only grandchild on my side. It meant she was a proper princess on Mum's side and was well looked after by my parents while I was at work. To balance it out, at Ted's parents, she was one of nine grandchildren which certainly kept her grounded. She has many happy memories of spending time there with her cousins.

Mum was a brilliant cook and Deborah remembers *always* having some form of meat, such as chops, chips and peas, or chops and cheese. As we are from Stoke-on-Trent, there were always Staffordshire oatcakes on the table, too! Mum's cooking was important for all of us and even the thought of her meals brings me back to her house. She made fresh ginger beer, with a bottle permanently in the larder containing a ginger beer plant; she baked incredible cakes, especially on Wednesdays, when she was always baking cakes and tray bakes ready for 'friendly hour' in church on Thursdays (a weekly event for seniors to gather and have a homecooked lunch); and her fabulous lamb roast with mint sauce on Sundays, complete with homemade puddings, was always a favourite. Ted and I also joined Mum for Sunday tea; a salad with salmon, followed by fruit cocktails and delicious, evaporated milk cream. A cream that we all love to this day. I believe Deborah is a regular consumer and always has some stock of it! Mum also made pickled cucumber and onion on Sunday, which got better with time, giving our meals during the week a delicious boost of flavours.

The more I grew, the more I appreciated just how kind Mum was. She was an innately nurturing person, always caring for other people and supporting her family. She was a born housewife who lovingly looked after every child she came into contact with, often looking after her friends' and neighbours' children, too, as well as Deborah and Dennis. Her house was therefore stocked with biscuits and homemade cakes – ready for her little guests; she often had more cakes than what could be consumed!

Mum loved cleaning and wouldn't stop until everything was shiny. Her house always smelled of lavender polish as a result. Nobody had filthy carpets or flooring when she was around, and she was always polishing her own oilcloth floors. Her house was warm and organised, and there was *always* washing around due to Mum's strict routines. She even helped with my housework on Friday evenings, particularly as I worked full-time, and especially as I wasn't so keen on cleaning! Upon reflection, Deborah must have got her love of cleaning from Mum; she certainly knew how to clean a house to immaculate standards after her time there. It seems that most of the passions and hobbies my family are proud of were inspired by one family member or another, passing down through the generations, whether it be DIY, gardening, fishing, cleaning, or wool crafts.

Where Mum was great at hosting and taking care of people, Dad was equally good at entertaining all of us. He loved playing the mouth organ or making everyone laugh with his jokes. He also had a dummy called 'Archie Andrews' and was brilliant with ventriloquism. This was most likely inspired by his best friend in The Royal Welsh Fusiliers who was *the* Punch and Judy man on Llandudno Pier, right up until Deborah was a young lady! Whenever we went to Llandudno, Dad couldn't get down to the pier fast enough to see him in action, and we still went down to the pier when the man's son took over the show in later years. Dad also made a Punch and Judy set, like a box theatre. All in all, Deborah had such good grandparents, both nurturing and entertaining.

I may not have had as big a passion for cleaning – and certainly not ventriloquism – but I loved sewing in my spare time. And as a young mum, I made day-to-day clothes or pretty dresses for Deborah to wear on special occasions. Sometimes, I also made matching outfits if I had spare material, but themed clothes or matching styles weren't common then, unlike when my grand-children were growing up.

Doreen, who lived with Mrs Hand, was also a very good tailoress.

We spent a lot of time together and enjoyed sharing ideas for making our daughters' clothes (she loved making beautiful clothes for her daughter Vicky). We spurred each other on to make clothes in new styles, and I must admit we could get competitive sometimes (though only in a friendly way!), especially as we had similar styles.

One time, I promised Deborah we would go shopping as a special treat and buy her a dress. Deborah was thrilled and we came home later with a beautiful new dress. Purely coincidentally, Doreen had also been out shopping and bought Vicky the exact same dress! We had a great laugh about it, and Deborah and Vicky loved being a matching pair.

Our Girl

W e enjoyed spoiling our Deborah with love, and we treasured having her around, actively encouraging her to come out with us whenever we went to Florence Club or elsewhere.

With Deborah being an only child, perhaps we worried more than the norm, but we didn't want anything to happen to her. The few scares we had were enough to stretch my anxiety to the limit! One story that comes to mind was how, as a little girl, Deborah fell on a plant pot in the garden and cut her wrist very deeply, just missing an artery. Thankfully she recovered quickly. But it seemed we couldn't be careful enough!

Deborah was a good daughter even through her teenage years. But I used to get so worried when she was out with her friends. I paced up and down in the house waiting for her to come back from wherever she was (usually the youth or church club). Sometimes, when she went to the Meir youth club with her friends on a Wednesday evening, I walked all the way there to check she was ok.

Deborah and I are very close, she was definitely a mummy's girl. We did so many things together that I couldn't capture them all, but some that stand out include when I took Deborah to the pictures to watch Batman. It was in glorious technicolour, and we were only used to a black and white TV. We were on the front row, and my eyes were never the same after that!

It was also lovely to have her friends over to our house for many sleepovers. Deborah was proud of her bedroom which Ted had decorated beautifully. She had a large room at the back of the house, with a double bed to herself, a huge fitted wardrobe, a record player, a beautiful dressing table Ted handmade, and other furniture that Ted had acquired, done up, and even sprayed gold. It was magnificent.

As mother and daughter, we spent many days doing embroidery together and knitting when Deborah was growing up. I also loved crochet, making some beautiful little crochet dresses. I taught her what I knew and to this day Deborah is an avid knitter, but she never enjoyed sewing and crocheting. Not all apples fall close to the tree!

Deborah also played the cello. Ted and I loved going to watch her play. They were always lovely occasions and we were both so proud of her. Ted would constantly talk about how good Deborah was at anything she did. And she really was very good at the cello, which she continued playing after leaving school. I will never forget one of her performances when she was really young, and all I could see were her two little legs around her enormous cello. It's one of those memories that will forever make me laugh.

Family Holidays
⌒〜〜⌒

Ted's family always wanted to go to Cornwall on holiday. As his mum didn't want to stay in hotels, we started our family holidays in farmhouses.

Later down the line, we preferred caravan holidays instead. Between Ted's four siblings, Mr and Mrs Hand, and ourselves, we would be in five caravans! It was like a wagon train with all his family going down there together.

As there were only three of us in our large caravan, we invited other nephews or nieces to stay with us. For example, Ted's brother preferred going on dancing holidays with his friends, so his two sons, our nephews John and Greg, often came with us. We loved having them there.

Everything used to go with us on these holidays. I mean *everything*. I can almost see my mother-in-law now, sitting in the back of her car with her coat and a hat on, with a little wooden box resting on her knee with her canary sitting in it. She used to bring the canary everywhere (she had a couple of canaries over the years, and they were *both* called Mr Spock!). Behind our car was a trailer filled to the brim with our belongings. One year, the wheel flew off the trailer on the motorway and sparks were flying everywhere. None the wiser, we were saying, 'What's happening there?' It wasn't long before we realised it was us causing the drama!

We loved caravanning for a couple of weeks in Newquay. Remembering, for context, this was in the 1960s and 1970s when it wasn't well known and serenely laid back and hippy, unlike today. Not many people there wore shoes, for example. It was brilliant.

Although we allowed ourselves to buy a Cornish pasty on one of the holiday days (because you can't go to Cornwall without that experience), we couldn't afford to eat out all the time. So, during the days, I took sandwiches to the beach or a flask of soup. I had one soup flask and one flask strictly designated for tea!

During the evenings, I cooked a simple tea in the caravan after which, occasionally, we went somewhere for a drink (keeping a beady eye on the children playing outside, of course).

As a special treat, one night of the holiday was singled out for a basket meal of chicken and chips. I know people eat out all the time these days, but it was a really special treat for us.

Ted's family was big and boisterous, and understandably there were sometimes disagreements during those holidays.

Ted was playing darts in a Newquay pub once when a stranger spilt a beer on his chair. Ted was not very happy and turned to the guy to say, 'Are you going to leave that there?'

A few too many drinks likely fuelled the fight that ensued. I went outside and left them to it. I wouldn't get involved in anything like that. The funny part of this story is that somehow Ted was completely unscathed! His sisters had stepped in to help, protectively, taking the brunt of some of the action themselves, with black eyes and their hair everywhere. The unbelievable part is that the stranger who caused it all in the first place was standing outside talking to me!

One night, I remember going out for a drink and taking all the kids with us. We were driving our cars between the pubs, always in a bit of a pickle in the back seat, clambering in and sitting on knees (back then, the rules for things like that were more relaxed). Anyway, when we were at the next pub we looked around and said, 'Where is John?' It transpired we had forgotten John, Ted's nephew, at the pub! We were miles away and hours had passed by without noticing. At that moment, whilst sitting in the beer garden, we saw the feather of the hat he always wore above the wall as he walked past it. He had walked all the way. It was a very comical moment, and we still laugh about it now.

Our holidays there were the same every year. If it rained, we stayed in and the men played cards. Deborah remembers how Ted used to say, 'Right, stand behind me for luck.' If it was raining outside, she was quite happy to sit next to her dad, playing cards.

A funny story that must get a mention is how even though two of Ted's sisters smoked, his mum wasn't supposed to know. One day, when they were cooking and cutting vegetables in one of the caravans, Ted's mum was seen heading over to them and they all quickly shoved their cigarettes into a half-cut cabbage!

We had such a marvellous time together and were all close friends. Though, I was especially close with Kathy, as I knew her from before I had even met Ted when I did piano lessons as a child.

Cornwall was such an important part of our lives. The first time we went to Cornwall with Ted was before we were married on a holiday with friends. Then, we went when I was expecting Deborah, and we continued going there every year after until Deborah was twenty-four years old.

Later down the line, Deborah went to Constantine with Ted, to see where he came from and learn about the family roots.

As a family, our life was all about great holidays and lots of family time. We made so many wonderful memories it would be impossible to capture them all.

Redundancies and Italian Football Shirts

Working full-time brought in more money for Ted and me. Within two years of my working in Tootles, we were able to buy a brand-new car and many other things which we wouldn't have been able to afford previously.

After staying several years at Tootles, I worked in a series of different sewing factories. They were large spaces with different floors and a cutting room where dozens of people worked. I enjoyed the work and met some wonderful friends there, some of whom I'm still friendly with now.

Most factories were in the local area, near our house, making it easy for me to commute to work on foot. Sometimes, though, I had to work in Tunstall or Leek, but they were only interim roles between more permanent roles in nearby factories. Working further away wasn't really an option for me as I didn't drive and suffered terribly from car sickness. So, even though at one point a mechanic from one of the factories kindly offered to give me lifts there and back, I couldn't do it as I was always sick on the journey!

Working in factories meant keeping up with fast-paced production work. We were often tasked with one part of a job, like sewing on the zips or fastening buttons onto garments. I must have been assigned hundreds of different tasks such as those in my time.

As this was the era when factories were being moved abroad to lower production costs, many – if not all – sewing factories in the UK closed their doors. This happened until the very end of my career when I was making clothes for Next. My colleagues and I were therefore among the last to work in such factories.

Due to this continuously changing scenario, I went from working in one factory to another and another in relatively short periods of time. There were never long gaps between jobs though, and I was often being made redundant on a Friday to receive a call that very night from another factory saying, 'Can you start on Monday?'

Overall, I was made redundant on about five or six occasions. It was frustrating at times, but some positives came with changing jobs. For example, I got to work on different styles of clothes, learning new techniques, and all the while broadening my experience using specialist machines.

In 1991 I was based in a factory where we made military uniforms, such as desert combat wear for soldiers during the First Gulf War. That was interesting, especially as we made uniforms for soldiers on both sides of the war! It was a strange but fascinating experience, often leaving me to wonder what the soldiers receiving those uniforms would come to face. With the military or government as our clients, we worked extra hard to ensure the quality of the products was impeccable, but it was far from ideal when it turned out that someone in our team had sewn the hoods on the wrong way for a whole batch of these uniforms, causing them to fall off! We worked hard to fix those issues as soon as we spotted them, of course. A very interesting moment during that period was the visit from someone who held high office in the team for President Arafat – a former Palestinian President and Nobel Peace Prize winner. His officials came to inspect the factory when considering our services. In fact, we often had visitors from people representing their companies or industries, but more often than not they weren't of great importance, so we carried on working as usual.

As much as I wasn't a football fan, it was fun to make hundreds of football shirts in another factory I moved to. There, companies like Nike or other sports brands signed contracts for large numbers of shirts or other sports clothes, and we fulfilled their orders. One time, we made the kit for the Italian football team, but to many people's disappointment, we never made the kit for our local team, Stoke. I enjoyed that job, and it was fun to see famous footballers wearing our clothes on the television!

A bonus of working in those factories was that during our lunch breaks we could use the machinery for our own personal projects. I used that time to make so many clothes for Deborah, Ted, and other children we knew. Using those specialist machines, such as a pressing machine, made all the difference for my projects. Not only did it speed up the production time, but it also made the clothes look much more professional. Besides, I simply wouldn't have been able to make some of the clothes had it not been for these machines; in the factory where I made military uniforms, for example, I had access to machines used to make denim clothes, so I made Ted some denim jeans and overcoats, too.

I enjoyed making all sorts of clothes, but I loved making dresses more than anything, especially for Deborah (and of course my grandchildren).

Later in my career, I went to work for Pippa Dee for many years, the party plan clothing factory, before going on to make clothes for Marks & Spencer, George at Asda, and Next. After a long, enjoyable career in sewing, I retired when I was sixty years old in 2000.

Working in these factories really honed my sewing skills. I have always enjoyed being crafty, but after my sewing career, I can't go shopping without looking at all the seams and seeing what has been done well or not.

I feel proud of the fact that I used my creative skills to make everything. I have loved being creative. I once embroidered a scene of Newquay (Tolcarne) beach, which we loved so much. It was huge! It hung on the wall of our lounge. I also made a mosaic lamp out of a bottle, which graced our lounge for many years.

I never bought anything and made everybody's clothes in the family. I used to make my husband's trousers, jackets, shirts. I made so many things. I made outfits for Deborah, and later for the grandchildren, too.

When Deborah married John in 1982, I didn't make her wedding dress, but we did choose her a lovely dress in a closing down sale, for £30, knowing that I could make something of it. I completely adapted it and, in the end, it looked entirely different!

Dancing Days

As I touched upon earlier, Ted and I loved dancing. In our thirties, Ted wanted to progress our dancing to the next level, so we began private dance classes in a nearby dance school. We would try out our new skills at our local working men's club called Florence Club.

Those lessons kindled a real love of dancing in me, and we learnt many of the Latin dances together. Ted was so good that he was always the best in the lessons! We made really nice friends in those classes, like Nora and Harry, who were really beautiful dancers. They remained friends with us through our dancing years and I am still close to them now.

Ted loved dancing so much that we used to go to the Florence Club to dance with friends on Thursday, Saturday, and Sunday nights. And when we weren't dancing, Ted played darts and I enjoyed socialising with friends and family in the main room, as Ted's sisters and brothers sometimes came with their children.

Deborah also joined us when she was older, and throughout her teenage years. We made countless happy memories there. Sometimes we also went to Stoke Town Hall and on special occasions like Christmas and for the New Year's Eve ball, we went to Trentham Gardens. I have some fantastic photographs of us at those dance events.

Ted and I continued dancing throughout our married life, particularly enjoying the Quickstep and Square Tango. We also enjoyed sequence dancing at Florence Club. We were really quite good, but we didn't participate in any competitions.

When I watch Strictly Come Dancing now, I can be quite critical, and Deborah says it is like sitting with one of the judges!

Another place we enjoyed going to in the evenings was Jollees, a live music and cabaret venue in Longton very close to where we lived. It was the biggest nightspot in the country back then, where all the big acts used to come and perform. We were so lucky to have it as our local, and we saw many brilliant musicians there.

Everyone really glammed up to go to Jollees, with the women always in long dresses. As I loved Shirley Bassey, I used to make drawings of her dresses and hand make them for our evenings out, which was good fun.

The evenings there were so well organised. We had to get tickets and reserve a table for supper and drinks, which was wonderful as the cabaret shows would play in front of you as you ate. The tables were always set in a beautiful way, with cosy lamps that made the space very atmospheric.

I always looked glamorous and adored having gorgeous dresses, which certainly wasn't a trait I inherited from my mum. My love of glamorous clothes definitely came from my grandma on Mum's side. Grandma liked jewellery, makeup, clothes, and all things glamorous. Whereas my mum dressed nicely, but she didn't like fancy things; one time I tried to convince Mum to wear Grandma's synthetic fur coat, but she couldn't do it, feeling terrible in it and worrying that if people saw her wearing it they would assume her to be posh and wealthy! She didn't like the feeling.

Flying the Nest

Deborah was such a lovely child. Her childhood years flew past and before we knew it, she was a young woman.

We had lived on Roxburghe Avenue for most of our lives, but when Deborah left home at twenty-one, we moved to a new bungalow on Chaplin Road, near to the park, where we stayed for the rest of our married life together.

It wasn't quiet when Deborah left, as I was always making clothes and sewing at work to return from work and do more sewing. We were also often busy doing up the bungalow. We always had a project going on in our house, as Ted and I loved DIY. In both homes, we extended and re-decorated, lovingly adorning each space. Ted was a real DIY man and worked magic in our homes. Credit where credit's due, not many people realised that I often had the ideas and Ted made them a reality! Anyway, we spent thirty-odd years in our bungalow and spent thirty-odd years doing it up.

Despite the fact we were so busy, I found it difficult without Deborah there and I got empty house syndrome. Saying that, Deborah and I do laugh whenever I bring this up as, rightly so, she reminds me that she only lived in her new house for eighteen months before moving to the road below our bungalow. She has never lived far away and I still see her every day.

Impossible Farewells

M y parents and parents-in-law all lived to ripe old ages. And yet many of Ted's family died well before their time. His sister, Doreen died in her forties, along with my sister-in-law, Margaret. Jack and Peggy died in their seventies.

So, although Ted had a large family to begin with, Kathy and I are the only ladies left now.

It has been such a tragedy for our family that so many relatives have died. We can't understand how we went from having such a large family to so few. It's like a cloud over us. I feel the heartbreak terribly – all of us do – and often wish they were here.

When Mark, Kathy's son, died it was dreadful. Deborah and Mark were the same age, and they grew up together, being born a few weeks apart. But when Mark turned twenty-one, he became ill and it turned out to be liver cancer. He died on 11 May 1983. It was an enormous sadness for our whole family.

Ted's parents lost their grandson, daughter, and daughter-in-law in an eighteen-month period. As I'm sure you can imagine, those years were the absolute worst.

Sadly, Auntie Emmie then died of breast cancer. Nobody knew she had it until after she died. She had kept it to herself. It was another huge loss.

Despite his accident, Dennis lived until the age of eighty-three, dying in 2014. He is greatly missed by all.

Our nephews, John and Greg, also passed away in recent years. The pain of young lives lost has been difficult to bear for those of us left behind.

Through all the sadness and grief, we take some comfort in knowing that we made so many special memories as a family.

There are countless events, holidays, family gatherings, and outings, and general day-to-day life, which we shared fondly. We cherish every single memory and remember those we lost through those memories. And, of course, the new additions to the family have helped bring so much joy. With James and Abigail, a new chapter began. It has been the best new chapter, and we loved having a lot of time with them.

The Joy of Grandchildren

I t was wonderful learning that we were going to become grandparents when Deborah told us she was expecting James.

James brought so much joy to our lives. The first time I held him was in the hospital when we went to meet him. When I saw him lying there, sleeping, it was so hard not to reach out and pick him up immediately. But it's never a good idea to wake a sleeping baby, and I remember Deborah saying, 'Don't disturb him, don't start him off crying!' He'd kept her awake all night.

James was a lovely baby and I have loved him from the moment I held him, to the man he has become today. He was a special baby who healed a lot of heartache for us, too.

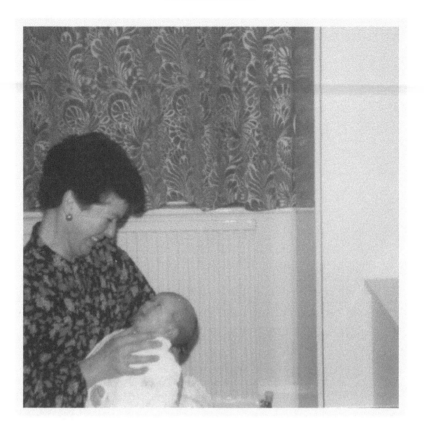

We just loved having a grandson. It was made all the more special by the fact that Ted would have loved to have a son; when I was pregnant, he often said, 'You're going to have a boy, I can feel it.' It never happened for us, of course, but the moment our James was born, we completely changed. We were thrilled.

A few years later, when James was two, Deborah had our second grandchild, Abigail, who we loved and adored. She was such a lovely baby and a good girl.

They have both brought so much joy to our lives. Deborah often jokes about the fact that when James and Abigail came along, the focus went off her and onto them!

I have such fond memories of going to bathe James and Abigail every night when they were little. Whatever shift Ted was on, I called at Deborah's on my way home from work to bathe the children while she cooked tea. It worked really well as an evening routine, giving me the opportunity to spend precious time with them. When Ted worked afternoon shifts, every other week, I went to Deborah's house after work and stayed later into the evening, enjoying a cup of tea with her while playing with the children.

Ted and I loved being grandparents and spent as much quality time with James and Abigail as we could throughout their childhood.

I carried on working until I was sixty, whereas Ted retired earlier. Because of this, he was able to help with school runs and child-care, as Deborah was back to working full-time by then. Ted collected them from school, made their tea and looked after them. Though, out of all the things he could have cooked them, I never worked out why he made them baked potatoes on bread and butter for their meals. That certainly wasn't from me! I used to make more wholesome meals like sausages, mash and peas. They always loved the food I made them.

Ted also looked after the children during their school holidays, which you will read about in the chapter Abigail has written for this book.

On weekends, I made up for the lost time by having the kids over to stay on Friday nights. We had too many wonderful evenings together to write about them all. While Ted went to the pub to have a drink, I stayed in with James and Abigail, cooking for them and spoiling them with love. We watched television together before bed, often watching films and programmes they probably shouldn't have been watching. At one point we enjoyed watching Eurotrash, which was definitely pushing it, given it could be quite rude. I don't think Deborah was so impressed to discover the things I let them watch! But we had a lot of fun.

The National Lampoon films were a real favourite of ours, too, and we watched a lot of those. At Christmas time, to this day, we still put those films on.

Continuing with tradition, I made so many clothes for the grandchildren and Deborah, often with matching fabrics! When Deborah was pregnant with Abigail, she had all her maternity dresses made by me, with James in a matching shirt. Later, Deborah and Abigail had dresses and James had shirts – all in the same material. There is a photo I love looking back on that shows the three of them in their matching clothes.

We went on many wonderful holidays in Devon, too, where we loved playing on the beach with kites and all sorts of other games. We also enjoyed playing table tennis in the evenings, getting dressed up to go for nice dinners, fishing on the beach (Ted was in charge of that!), and cooking the fresh catch of mackerel for meals.

Christmas was also special, with Deborah and her family coming over to ours for dinner and festivities. I decorated the house so much that the grandkids said it looked like Santa's grotto!

I loved being silly with James and Abigail. Perhaps I got it from James, or the other way around, as James continually entertained us when we looked after him, always being the practical joker. It would be impossible to try and count the practical jokes he played on us. He was a real comedian, always ready with a box of jokes and tricks. He brightened our days and made us laugh so much. Saying that, he could be a monkey at times!

A Special Boy

I love James. He is very special to me and he was very special to his grandad as well. We spoilt him and gave him so much love. Even now, I give him a big kiss when I see him. He's always been very affectionate with us, and we cuddled up on the sofa many nights, telling funny jokes to each other.

James and Ted had the most special of bonds and James had a very special place in Ted's life. Ted was James' number one supporter in life, always wanting to make sure he was ok.

Ted had always loved fishing. In fact, he loved fishing so much that when we got married there was an article in the local paper with the headline, 'Fisherman Gets Hooked For Life'. People often announced their marriages in the papers in those days, but I wonder how many had a headline like that! There was a lovely picture of us in that article, which I still have somewhere.

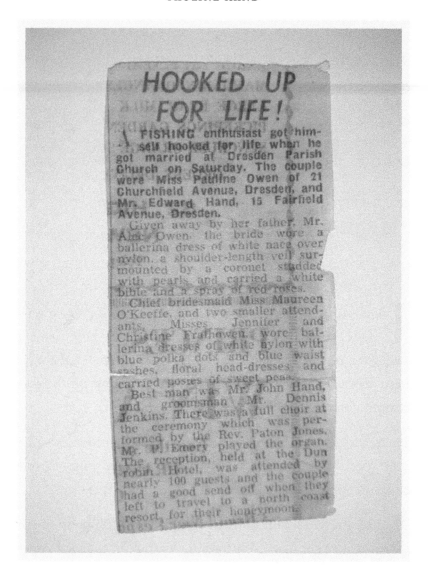

A few decades later, when James came along, fishing became even more special. As grandad and grandson, they spent a lot of time fishing, turning it into their favourite pastime. They fished together on holidays, often catching our tea, with Abigail joining in, too. James and Ted also fished locally, getting passes to local lakes and rivers. That continued right up until Ted died. At the very end, James and Ted would go carp fishing, even when Ted wasn't very well. Another thing they enjoyed together was playing a good game of chess and backgammon. They really were as close as best friends.

James is now an electrician and he is very good at his job. He is also a lovely dad to Grace, who is very similar to him. Grace is so funny, and he adores her. I hope he continues to take care of himself, being a good husband and father, as he is now. If he grows to be anything like Ted, I know he won't go far wrong.

Ambitious and Kind: Our Abigail

A bigail is just lovely. I have always been very close to her, and Ted and Abigail adored each other.

Abigail and I have a lot in common. She is very similar to me. We both enjoy fashion, clothes, and makeup, and we *love* shopping. We often go shopping together, with Deborah coming along to have a coffee, too (she is not as keen on shopping!).

Abigail was always good as a child. She was studious as well, constantly reading and entertaining herself. She was also good company and you can't say that of all children. She has become kind, generous, and incredibly ambitious – that is definitely the word for her! In any situation, she knows what to say and what to do at the right moment. She also makes the best out of any situation she is in, always bouncing back. She is one of those people who knows how to take action and move forwards in life.

Seeing her get married was very special. She looked beautiful. And despite the fact it was raining on the day, with everyone under umbrellas, the wedding was lovely.

We have always remained close, speaking to each other on the phone when we can't see each other. And I love going to see my great-grandchildren now. They are lovely.

Abigail has achieved so much. She is one of life's winners. We are so proud of her. And she is so wonderful with her children. I hope she continues what she's doing because she's doing very well.

She has often been very generous and treated me to special things. Most memorably, one time she took me to an evening with Sylvester Stallone, as she knows I like him (well, she knows I especially love his mother, Jackie Stallone!). As an older lady who always looks so glamorous, Jackie has always been someone I admire. Abigail paid for special tickets at this event which allowed us to ask a question. Well, for me the question was simple. I asked Sylvester, 'How's your mother?'

Abigail and James are both doing ever so well. They were both good and lovely children, and now they are lovely parents. My hope and message to them for their future is:

Do unto others as you would have done unto yourself.

Don't be nasty with anybody.

If you can be kind, be kind, and you will get kind deeds returned.

Green Fingers and My Plant Hospital

T his book couldn't go without a chapter on gardening because it has been extremely important to me through the years.

Gardening has been a lifelong passion of mine. I'm not able to do so much now, as the place where I live has a tiled garden and my plants are, therefore, all in tubs. But years ago, I loved spending time in my garden, seeing plants and flowers being nurtured and growing.

Whenever I see someone's plant looking like it's going downhill, I say, 'Let me take that to my plant hospital and get it back on its feet for you.'

I have been running a plant hospital forever, and have always loved looking after plants, getting them back to strength. I do this by talking to the plant, removing old leaves, and caring for it until it recovers. I've always done that. I just love plants and I still have many in the house now.

Hazel, my dear friend who you will read about in chapters to follow, has often given me plants that needed reviving, asking me to heal them in my plant hospital.

Gardening is a brilliant hobby. It gives you time to think and process daily life and stresses while also giving you a routine, with the planting schedules at the different times of the year. I had a potting shed, so I was always looking ahead; preparing bulbs for the next season and putting seeds in the soil (I used to grow everything from seed!). We had flowers and green plants all year round, with about thirty hanging baskets around our detached bungalow! Everyone used to stop and look at our flowers.

I also enjoyed growing fruits and vegetables, always giving bags of tomatoes away when I often harvested more than we could eat.

Visiting beautiful gardens and parks was something I enjoyed very much when I could walk more easily. I have been on many trips to National Trust gardens and particularly loved looking around the various greenhouses. As we lived near Trentham Gardens, I loved looking around there and seeing what they had. I often walked around the area where they sold plants, buying new seeds and flowers on my way. I still go there now to have a little look. When I go on holiday with Deborah and her husband in their caravan, I also enjoy going to the garden centre nearby, looking at all the arrangements of flowers and pots. As I can't resist a plant, I always fill the car with them on the way home!

I have always loved roses and rose trees, and wherever I lived I had roses over my front door. In my previous house, it was a beautiful red rose.

Among the many plants I have loved and tended to, there is one that couldn't be more special. When my grandma died, Mum wasn't interested in inheriting jewellery or anything material belonging to her mother. Instead, she went into Grandma's garden with a shovel, carefully digging a plant out of the flower bed, before carrying it all the way home. This plant was Mum's special way to remember her mother. To carry on the tradition, when my mum died, I went and did the same thing in Mum's garden, taking that very plant to remember her by. It was a beautiful, old-fashioned plant, and it remained in my garden ever since. When we moved, I brought it to our bungalow. It also came with me when I moved to the house I live in now, where it happily lives in one of my many pots (though exactly which pot I couldn't be sure!). I also got the red rose tree from Grandma's garden, too.

I was only eight when I lost my grandma, but I continued lovingly tending to these flowers my whole life.

Travelling Abroad

◆◆◆

Ted and I didn't go abroad until much later in life. When we were young it wasn't such a common thing, and it never crossed our minds because we loved going to the places we knew. When Ted's parents died and we stopped going to Cornwall, we began visiting Devon with Deborah and the children instead. We never felt like we missed out by not going abroad, as our holidays were wonderful.

When Deborah was in her forties, she went abroad for the first time and she had a lovely time. At the same time, Ted and I were invited by his cousin Eileen to go to Tenerife. I was sixty by that point and we were both stuck in our ways. But Deborah convinced us to try it, fuelled by her recent holiday. There was no turning us back after that! We had a wonderful time and Ted fell in love with Tenerife.

I will never forget coming out of the airport for the first time and seeing all the palm trees. I had only ever seen them in pictures. It was a sunny day and as I acclimatised to the new scenery and heat, I remember thinking that everything was just as lovely as I had imagined it to be.

Given it was our first time abroad, everything was very exciting. Eileen's apartment had a banana plantation behind it that fascinated me, never having seen anything like it. The apartment itself was very swanky, too, which we enjoyed. We also went out for meals and I tried new and delicious foods, but that wasn't so fun for Ted who could be a fusspot with his food! He wouldn't eat any food other than what he knew, so going out for a meal was never on his to-do list. He loved my cooking, my dinners, and a pudding. That was it. He only liked proper English food, and I couldn't get him to order anything like spaghetti or foreign-sounding meals. In restaurants, he fiddled with his food, pretending to eat it, before going out to look for a chip shop... Luckily, we found a chip shop wherever we were, and we ended up going there to buy his meals.

Aside from the food, we absolutely loved going to Tenerife and went twice a year in the winter for ten years, going for my birthday in March and Ted's birthday in November.

Ted's cousin was delighted and glad for the company. We stayed with her the first trip before staying in hotels on the following visits. We went to different places and hotels each time, but we particularly loved Los Christianos. I loved going around the huge open market there, enjoying the many colourful stalls filled with things you would never have found in England.

Being real sun worshippers, we spent long days sunbathing and relaxing on the beach. When not on the beach we were walking and exploring different areas. Every day, we walked from Playa de las Americas all the way along to the next town. It was a leisurely walk along the beachfront, stopping at a bar where I had a 'pop' and Ted enjoyed a pint of beer. I also spent a lot of time shopping, of course, as there were delightful shops all along the front.

Ted

Until the day he died, Ted tried to keep healthy, fit, and active. He enjoyed going out for a pint with his brother or brothers-in-law a couple of times a week, commonly on a Friday or Saturday night. Ted's two best friends married two of his sisters, so they remained very close throughout their lives. In better days they also watched live football matches when Stoke was playing. Our whole family was very close.

When Ted was diagnosed with non-Hodgkin's lymphoma, it was a really hard time for us as individuals and as a couple. The hardest thing to come to terms with was being told the cancer had spread after he had been in remission. We had been so relieved before that devastating news.

When Deborah explained to me that Ted only had between five weeks and five months to live, just after they had discovered the cancer had spread to his brain, it was too much to cope with. It was a truly terrible time. But I somehow pulled myself together and we did our best as a family to make Ted as comfortable as possible.

Ted died at home with Deborah, Ray, and me by his side on 16 November 2010, a few days before he would have turned seventy-three years old. The whole family came to pay their respects afterwards. He was so loved, and his death was devastating to everyone who loved him.

The day Ted died my world changed forever. In our marriage, Ted was the decision-maker. He paid the bills, sorted our correspondence, and organised so many of the important things. It was the way our marriage worked, always finding a balance between us. We shared a lifetime of memories. A lifetime of love. Losing him was incomprehensible.

The big sadness was also that so many of the good things happened after Ted died in 2010. He wasn't there to witness everything he wanted to see; the first great-grandchild was born less than a year later; Abigail and James got married within a year of each other; and Grace, James' little girl was born not long after, on James' first wedding anniversary.

Everything that happened was lovely and it has been wonderful to meet the great-grandchildren, but it has all been bittersweet without Ted around.

Life After Ted

L ife after Ted has not been easy, but I knew I couldn't let the grief be the end of my life.

When Ted died, people expected me to fall apart, and the first few days were indeed very dark. But even then, I knew the best thing to do when going through grief was to remember that I was still here. You simply have got to carry on.

Deborah stayed with me the first night after Ted passed away and then asked me if I wanted to go and stay at her house for a while, as she didn't want me to be alone. But I didn't want to because I knew I had to get on with it. I had to get myself right and get myself together, and I did just that. Perhaps Deborah is correct when she says I am tough as nails, just like my cousin Andrew had told her reassuringly when Ted died. Apparently, he'd said, 'I've known your mother longer than you. Your mother is tougher than you think.'

So, as hard as it was, I carried on.

A poignant moment for me was when I turned to Deborah and said, 'We don't belong to each other Deborah. We're on loan to each other.'

When we lose someone close to us, it is my firm belief that we need to accept this fact, hard as it may be. All of us are only on loan to each other.

Having family close by was important during those tough years, particularly with Deborah and Abigail living nearby, having moved after Ted died. We have been so close as a family, going through each high and low together.

Deborah and I still live a few doors away from each other and she has supported me with many things. I have never had to cook for myself since Ted died, for example, as I always eat at Deborah's house.

The house is quiet without Ted around but I fill the time with seeing family, friends, and enjoying my crafts. With clothes being so cheap to buy now, I don't sew anymore, but I enjoy knitting while watching the television (I would go to sleep if I just sat there watching the television!). The great-grandchildren always have beautiful handknitted cardigans as a result.

Deborah and I love knitting and always have a project on the go, spending many pleasant evenings knitting together. In the past, I made up the garments for her and would often tell her, 'You've got to start sewing up, I can't sew up the garment for you forever!'

In a perfect role reversal, I now knit cardigan after cardigan but leave Deborah to sew them up. We have such hearty laughs about this now. Nonetheless, I do still mother her now, even though she does a lot of the caring for me.

Hazel: A New Chapter

Hazel is a very good friend who came into my life when I needed her. Before Ted died, she was living across the road from our bungalow on Chaplin Road. Although we had seen each other around, we hadn't been close friends (only because we hadn't crossed paths much). If anything, Hazel knew Ted more than she knew me, as she used to go to the pub with her husband, Stan, where they often saw Ted.

Hazel had recently lost her own husband, too, when Ted died. She knew what I was going through and so she came over to my house to ask how I was doing. Little did we know back then that such a tight bond would form between us.

Not only did we have similar circumstances, but we are the same age and have a lot in common. We have almost lived parallel lives. It wasn't long before she became a dear friend of mine. She is so good to me.

Instead of curling up in a ball when we became widows, we got together and went for it; going out and living our lives, starting a whole new chapter together.

When two bungalows were put on sale on Rugby Drive where we live now, Hazel and I bought them together so that we could live next to each other. We see each other all the time. We spend so much time together that Deborah has switched from saying 'Mum and Dad' to 'Mum and Hazel'!

Among many things we have done, Hazel and I have been on lovely holidays to Spain and Tenerife. We have also been on trips to Bournemouth, Torquay, and Llandudno. Frustratingly, the pandemic meant we haven't been able to travel abroad, and I don't think we will ever go again. But it hasn't stopped us from enjoying our lives, even with some added difficulties.

Tenerife 2015

When everyone feared going out in the early days of the pandemic, we persevered and still went out when we could and when things opened. In fact, we caught covid from each other after the first wave! We were both fortunate enough to recover, though it took longer for me as I was more poorly with it.

We still have a lovely time together; having meals every week and often calling by each other's houses for a chat. Every Wednesday, we get a taxi and go somewhere different for a meal with Pam and Ivy, two other good friends, and we have a brilliant evening out. We also go to town during the day. As I can't walk around so much, I sit and wait in the car while Hazel goes around the shops, and then we have a coffee together.

I'm so grateful for Hazel. She has been such a good friend and meant a lot to me since I have been on my own. I appreciate her and our friendship very much.

The One Regret

ᏩᏭᎤ

I try to make the most of every day. Perhaps it is for this reason that I don't think there is anything I would change about my life, except for the fact I would have liked to learn how to drive. I do wish I could drive now.

Apart from the time I drove an old boyfriend's car as a teenager, when I shouldn't have been driving, I didn't learn. Ted was kind and drove me everywhere instead.

Though, when the drink driving laws came into place Ted did try to teach me. It would have been handy for pub runs, given I never liked drinking anyway. He cheekily turned to me and said, 'Do you know, I think it would be nice if you could drive!'

I believe one driving lesson was all Ted could cope with after the scare I gave him... We got in the car, with me in the driver's seat, and Ted guided me down the road. Everything was going relatively ok, but even so, Ted was very anxious. When I looked at him, there was sweat running down his face. I persevered and tried to learn, but that didn't last for long. I was overtaking a car when Ted saw a lorry coming towards us. He quickly explained how I needed to get through the gap. Suddenly, feeling quite afraid, I just closed my eyes and put my foot down. Ted was sweating with fear when we got safely to the other side. That was the beginning and the end of my driving.

Lockdown Reflections

❧

G oing through the war makes you appreciate many things. I am always grateful for the simple things in life now, such as being able to put nice food on the table and to buy nice clothes. We should never take anything for granted.

I find it frustrating to hear people in the UK complaining about not having enough money. If they had been through what we experienced in the war, with rations continuing into the 1950s, I doubt they would be complaining. Of course, that's not to say all cases are the same, but generally, everyone now has *something* compared to what we had. We didn't even have the NHS until 1948; when you went to the doctor you had to pay. Often people didn't have any money and couldn't go. The situation back then was very different. It really isn't so bad now with regards to accessing financial or other support.

On the other hand, people often tell me how resilient we all were to get through the war days. But people can forget how resilient they are now. I definitely feel that what we went through with the covid-19 pandemic and subsequent lockdowns was worse than the war days for some reasons. For example, during the war, you had your family support around you. Regardless of the fear that was part of daily life, the experience felt different because we had each other. We were living as family units in close-knit communities, in contact every day. During lockdowns, we didn't have each other in the same way.

Many people in my generation are not tech-savvy, not knowing how to use Zoom and modern smartphones or tablets. That made it hard to communicate with the outside world when we were stuck at home. This was the case for me, especially during the initial, stricter lockdown. Even though I had a tablet, I couldn't use it. The loneliness has been very destructive for the elderly. Not to mention the fear and anxiety brought on by the news, especially around the start of the pandemic.

Nonetheless, we have to persevere and carry on, whatever happens. And that we did. As soon as it was possible, I was going out again, seeing family and friends.

The Power of Faith

⮑◈⮐

B eing a Christian, whenever I face a difficult situation I always pray about it, leaving any problems with God. I firmly believe we need to leave our problems at the foot of the cross. It is something I have always done and, usually, things turn out alright.

As a Christian I have always gone to church and believed in a good, clean life. I believe there is a plan for everybody.

Mum taught me that God always has the answer. She said that everything would be fine because of this, and it always was for her. Like mother, like daughter, I have carried this belief forwards and it has helped me throughout my life. That is why, whatever happens, I always try to be positive knowing that everything happens for a reason. If something goes wrong, it's because it is meant to be and there is something better for you. If you lose your job, for example, it's because there is a better one around the corner for you. We need to keep believing that everything will turn out ok in the end. When Deborah recently lost her little dog, for example, it was very sad, but I knew she would be ok, 'He's had a wonderful life.' I said to her, 'You'll be ok. Everything's going to be fine.'

It's just in my nature to see life through this lens.

Thanks to my Christian upbringing and my lovely mum, I have always had a caring and nurturing side to my character. I also learnt some important values and lessons that I wanted to share:

Look after your home and your children.

Be kind to your children. You will want them to be kind to you when you are older.

Be careful and don't do too much of anything. Don't drink too much. Just do things moderately and live moderately.

Be kind where you can be kind. Do unto others as you would want to be done unto yourself.

Lead a good, clean life: if you behave yourself, you will be ok.

Have **joy** in your life, and remember this:

Jesus first

Others second

Yourself last.

Most importantly, remember that the Everlasting Arms are underneath you, and round about you, so you will never hit rock bottom.

These values and motivations have been part of my life and shaped how I have lived.

Paddle Your Own Canoe

Another thing that is very important in life is to be independent. It isn't good to always depend on other people. That is why I have helped family in any way I can but not financially. It sounds harsh, but it is a good learning curve.

People should stand on their own two feet and paddle their own canoe. Our Deborah always did, and she learnt to do it herself. She lived on her own for many years with her children and was fine. I know we have shared that philosophy in our parenting styles.

I also believe that people should have their own homes. They shouldn't be living with their parents for too long. Even a mother bird chucks out her chicks when the time comes. Independence is key in life and this is the philosophy I have lived by.

Ted and I worked hard in the hope that future generations in our family did better than us. I am proud of how independent

Deborah, Abigail, and James are, working hard and owning their own homes.

I would like to finish by saying that we need to live our life. Despite my age, I certainly haven't stopped having fun. I still enjoy being silly with the grandchildren and great-grandchildren. I believe there was even a video of me added to Facebook proving this in 2017, showing me whizzing around the house on a hoverboard one of the children got for Christmas. I have never stopped trying new things. We only live once, after all!

Thank you for reading this book. I have enjoyed the process of recalling my life story. Although I have never been a keen reader, I will certainly read this book.

An Idyllic Childhood

BY DEBORAH

MY DAD'S EARLY YEARS

My dad, Ted, grew up in Stoke-on-Trent. His parents had five children and my dad and his twin, Kathy, were the youngest in the family. With his dad working in the pit, it would have been a busy time for his mum.

My dad's first holiday was at the age of seventeen when he went to Blackpool for a weekend with his friends, who later became his brothers-in-law. He met Mum the week after, when he was eighteen, which you will know about from having read my mum's story.

From the beginning, family were so important to my parents and they especially loved their nephews and nieces. Dad's eldest sister, Auntie Peggy, had a son called Andrew who would have been seven or eight when my parents were courting, and they were very close. Dad and Mum never went on a date without him, and he would sit between them in the cinema. 'He was a nuisance,' Dad used to say affectionately, 'He wouldn't let us sit together.'

Star Hotel, South Promenade, Blackpool.

In the early days of their relationship, they went fishing together, too, as Dad loved fishing. My mum would tie a bit of string to a stick for Andrew, and surprisingly, they caught a fish like that!

Andrew became Dad's go-to person and confidant as the age gap narrowed over time. They were more like brothers, on par with best friends, rather than nephew and uncle. Andrew's wife, Linda has been a marvellous addition to the family, too. Andrew's sister, Gail is Mum's much-loved goddaughter. Mum had no siblings but there were four girls and five boys in my dad's family to love and enjoy. She really loves all her nephews and nieces, and they all love her.

Dad was so close to his brothers and sisters even though they often disagreed, very loudly, through big arguments that meant nothing! There would be an argument one minute and in the next minute it would all be forgotten. Coming from a smaller, more peaceful household, she thought it was strange, but over time she became part of the family, too.

I have a lovely photograph that encapsulates my dad's family, with everybody together, really laughing. In fact, they always did everything together as a family, so when family members died later down the line, it was devastating. Sadly, we have lost too many, too soon.

GROWING UP IN POST-WAR BRITAIN

I was born sixteen years after the end of the war, in 1961, only five years or so after the end of rationing. In post-war Britain, there was very little spare money. Families depended on each other.

My parents were so driven to pay the mortgage, and they worked hard to do so. I remember we couldn't have extra things until they had paid it off, which happened when I was nine years old. They were very hardworking and gave me the best childhood.

THE HEAD OF THE FAMILY

Dad was a real character. He always saw the downside of anything. If you were going to buy a car, for example, he read about that car, learning all the things that were wrong with it, putting a dampener on it, so that you bought the car he was recommending. He could be like that. 'You shouldn't buy that one.' He would say.

When I was born, my dad registered my birth. My mum had wanted me to be called Susan Jayne, but he called me Deborah Jayne. Coincidentally, the same happened with my own daughter, Abigail. She was meant to be called Hilary, and I still have her little hospital name tag to prove it!

My dad was very much the head of our family and we all went to him for advice. He advised everyone on everything. He would know so much, from finance to books on DIY. He could do anything; you name it and he did it himself. He built his own extension on the bungalow, built his own garage, put roofs up, tiled, and fitted a kitchen.

He always had advice for younger members of the family, too. Everyone looked up to him. We all remember his advice to this day, and we even had a recording of him talking to my son, James, after he bought a new phone. You can hear my dad saying, 'Now every time you use it, you must put it back in your pocket.' He didn't want James to lose it.

As much as he gave advice, he also didn't miss opportunities to prove he was right. It makes me smile now, remembering how if anything ever went wrong, he had always predicted it in advance.

He never did anything wrong. We used to call him Mr Perfect. He even had some slippers with 'Mr' on one slipper and 'Perfect' on the other.

If you lost something, he would say, 'Urgh. These people! I have never lost a thing in my life.'

Recently, I found myself saying the same thing to my friend Jill. I was brought up to look at everything practically, so I'm like my dad. Though, in some ways, I wish I was more like my mum. She's so sweet-natured, whereas Dad was more direct.

Though, it must be mentioned that even though all big decision-making was left to Dad, Mum told me how she used to get her own way on everything. Nobody ever realised it. She used to make Dad believe it was his idea! She had this knack of using her womanly wiles, and she always had a way with my dad, bringing him around on a subject, usually DIY-related, as she often wanted to knock the house about.

I know my mum misses my dad – Ted – very much. Losing him was so hard for all of us.

HARD TIMES

I had plenty to be happy about as a child. I had lovely parents, a lovely home, lovely grandparents, and eight cousins. It was just lovely, and we spent a lot of time together as a family. I know we all value what we shared to this day. But things were not always easy, and there was a sad period when I was a little girl.

As you would have read earlier in this book, Mum and Dad had always intended to have a family of children. Sadly, in 1963, my mum had a baby who only lived for a few hours. Then, in 1964, she had a stillbirth. That had a very profound effect on her life, casting a shadow over them both, and Mum has suffered lifelong depression since. Dad came from a big family, and he found it very hard, too, as a large family was really important to him.

As a child, I knew something was going on, even though none of this was mentioned at the time. I remember my mum sitting me down on the stairs and showing me a box of baby clothes, as well as baby toiletries, explaining that we were going to be having a new baby in the house. But it never happened. I didn't remember this until years later when we talked about it more recently after Dad died.

In 2014, it was the fiftieth birthday of one of those babies. Mum knew where the first baby was buried, even though she had been too upset to go to the funeral at the time. She thought the second baby had been incinerated at the hospital. So, in 2014, I decided it was important to get a stillbirth certificate for that child, so that we could name him and put the name on the gravestone where the first baby is buried. When I rang the registrar to get a certificate, they told me the baby hadn't been incinerated at the hospital. He was buried in the same grave with the first baby. My mum hadn't known this for fifty years because nobody told her, not wanting to upset her. When I tried to tell her in 2014, she couldn't accept it at first; she had been going to this grave all these years and both babies had been in there all along.

Mum and I spoke and agreed this should go in this book, especially to help people going through anything similar now. Back then, when she went through this, nobody spoke of these things. That resulted in her suffering from depression for fifty years. It had been a taboo subject for too long.

FATHER AND DAUGHTER

My mum was more of the loving one between my parents, whereas my dad was very strict when I was growing up. I was completely wrapped in cotton wool as my parents didn't want anything to happen to me, as they only had me. I wasn't allowed a bike to ride, to go palaces with friends, or do anything risky. That was a bone of contention with me, but I knew the boundaries and I never asked twice. I didn't always like the things Dad said to me and vice versa. But I did adore my dad. We were so alike. Actually, I would say we are exactly the same.

Dad did shift work in the pit, so it was difficult to have times when we all sat together as a family. But I did used to pop in when he came back from work at night. I remember him always having tea and toast for breakfast and the same for supper when he came in, even on the later shifts that we called the noon shift, when he got home at ten o'clock.

I was scared when Dad worked there. My friend's dad had been killed in the pit and that had been heavy on my mind. I used to be scared until he returned home, sighing with relief when I heard the door shut.

Our relationship wasn't the stereotypical father-daughter relationship. Although he would help me with homework and support me in everything, I was definitely a mummy's girl at heart.

If I wasn't very well, he always used to come and rub my head, ruffling my hair. That was a big loving gesture from my dad. My mum used to tease him, saying that when someone was ill, he didn't know what else to do. But that was his way of showing love and affection. Even now, if I feel poorly, I can feel him doing this. I miss him very much.

Dad and I had our own special bond. Something I remember fondly is how even when I was a big girl, he always carried me up to bed as I fell asleep downstairs every night. My mum would say, 'You'll be able to carry him one day!'

There are so many fond memories I have with my parents. And travelling to our many holidays, often in Llandudno or Cornwall, will always be among my fondest. The journey in the car with my parents and usually a few others was always brilliant (something Abigail experienced in later holidays, too!). My mum got so car sick and my dad would give her a sick bag to avoid pulling over. She took travel sickness tablets, which always made us laugh, as she slept for hours after taking those pills. I always loved those journeys, with Mum trying to read the map while nodding off to sleep, while my dad would get so frustrated. It would really make me laugh.

We went to Cornwall for many years because when Dad found a place he liked, he got stuck in his ways and never wanted to go anywhere else. We had such great times on holiday.

My dad always loved playing games on the beach with his nephews, nieces, and brothers-in-law, who were his best friends. He always took a bodyboard with him to surf on, and he had what he called a jockery set; a wooden box with a long piece of elastic that had a small tennis ball on the end. We spent many hours playing with that on the beach.

As a child, I liked running and was quite good at it at school, winning some of the races. I remember how on our holidays Dad trained me and I ran all along the beach holding his hand.

I have fond memories from our Christmas mornings, too. First, we opened my presents in the morning, with Mum and Dad taking photos on their camera. Later, when they had a reel-to-reel recorder, they also recorded me, playing the video back to all and sundry. After this, we went to Grandma's house (on my dad's side), and I was allowed to take a few presents with me to show Grandma and Grandad. Grandma always had little glasses of Drambuie lined up for all the visiting family. It is my absolute favourite drink to this day, which my mum can't believe, as she used to dread it so much it made her toes curl. But it brings back so many memories for me. It's definitely my favourite tipple.

Following that, we went to my maternal grandparent's house for Christmas dinner. We stayed there all afternoon and had tea, before going to auntie Doreen's house – Dad's sister who tragically died really young – where we had a great party with all the family gathered. It was always very special. I was spoilt at Christmas and on my birthdays.

Another thing that stands out in my memories is how Dad loved playing cards, and how I often stood next to him while he played. He was a brilliant darts player, too, and he played in local darts teams. He won lots of trophies, which were always proud moments, but he had so many we had to give some away. When a celebrity darts player came to play locally, he loved going along to watch the games, and when they asked someone from the audience to play, he would be the one to raise his hand. My dad was good, and he won! Darts really was my dad's thing. He was just utterly brilliant at it. My mum was always proud of him, and she would go with him if there were darts finals in the area, cheering him on. Inspired by him, I went on to play darts later down the line, and I was in a lady's team.

My mum was a lovely mum, and I always had beautiful clothes because she made all my clothes, even my coats. I just had the loveliest parents, grandparents, and cousins (I was one of nine!), and I was spoilt by my grandma on my mum's side, as she only had me as a grandchild. It really was fabulous, with lots of family, lots of love on both sides. It was just idyllic.

GRANDCHILDREN AND RETIREMENT

Things happen for a reason. Nana lost what she said was a little boy before she had my mum, after falling from height on a ladder. Then Mum lost two boys and Dad was desperate to have a boy.

When I had James, it made up for all of it. All the hurt my parents had been through was over the minute James was born. Dad had his wish. James was Dad's best friend until the day he died. He adored him, and I have always been so happy to have been able to give my parents that joy.

There is one photo, showing my mum looking down at James when he was born, that brings me back to that special moment. He was everything to them because of what they had lost. He changed our whole lives. It is very emotional to think back to it now.

When I was pregnant again, I remember my dad saying, 'I really hope you get a girl this time, I think everyone should get a daughter.'

Abigail was born not long afterwards.

When I had my children, things really livened up for my parents. It opened a massive new chapter. The best chapter. And my parents felt what it was like to have a family. I always shared my children with them and that was wonderful. Really, they were like another set of parents to James and Abigail. They were overjoyed, being really involved and relaxed. They loved grand-parenting.

James and Abigail slept at my parent's house every Saturday night, and they spent lots of time together, as I was working full-time. It was brilliant.

When Dad retired from work about twelve years before Mum, who continued working full-time until she was sixty, he looked after the kids during the holidays. He also helped with school runs. My children will be able to recall more memories of this period.

A special memory, looking back, was when Michelin put on a lovely retirement party for Dad. I was there with James and Abigail, and it was a real family occasion. They had a photographer and we have a lovely family photo from that event.

My dad was a very fit and healthy man. Even in his retirement, he always looked younger than his age. When he collected my kids from school, people used to think he was my husband! Even in his seventies, he looked like he was in his fifties. He was just young in his outlook, working out in his garden gym every day.

FAMILY HOLIDAYS WITH THE GRANDCHILDREN

We went on family holidays with my parents, and when James and Abigail were born, we found a place in Devon by accident. We loved it so much it became our go-to place for ten years. Torcross is in the Dartmouth region, and we just loved the River Dart. Mum's godparents, Auntie Winnie and Uncle Hubert (the Smiths) lived there, so we had visited when I was younger.

We stayed at the Apartment Hotel in Torcross, which was lovely. We always took table tennis bats with us, as the kids enjoyed playing table tennis in the games room in the evenings. It was quite funny because there was a fruit machine in the games room and Abigail was extremely good on it. She has known how to make money since she was a tot! She was only little, but she worked out how to win on this machine, and people were paying her to play. She was coming home with more money than she went with. We realised then that she was a little entrepreneur!

James and Abigail loved fishing. In fact, James and my dad have been lifelong friends and companions through fishing. When the children were young, they used to do beach casting with fishing rods. Abigail was a good fisherwoman, too. They used to catch mackerel that I cooked in the microwave back at the apartment.

We had a great time on holiday, going on beautiful days out every day. We used to go into Torquay for the day, have some fun there, and then head into Dartmouth. There was a café we used to love having breakfast at, al fresco, which was ahead of its time, being very trendy. Despite this being years ago, it would still be modern today.

In August, we went to a holiday camp in either Exeter, Cornwall, Devon, or somewhere else down south. My father won the darts tournament every single time on those holidays, winning us all a free holiday in October.

There also used to be a finals tournament in these holiday camps for all the people who won the darts titles, the week before the parks closed at the end of the season. My dad won every year. We were proud to be with him, and my mum was always just right behind him. Those were such nice times that we had.

By the time Mum was sixty, I finally managed to persuade my parents to go abroad for a holiday in Tenerife. I was overjoyed when they went. My parents fell in love with Tenerife and in their later years – their last ten together – they had many holidays there. Once they found Tenerife, they didn't go anywhere else!

THE END OF AN ERA

In 2009, Dad was diagnosed with non-Hodgkin's lymphoma.

Dad had always kept fit before his diagnosis. In fact, when the doctors asked him if he exercised, he told them, 'Oh yes, I still like to look good on the beach on my holidays.' He meant it, too.

Although he made a full recovery after treatment, with a full remission, the cancer had silently spread to his brain – an area that hadn't been covered by the chemotherapy.

Dad died on 16 November 2010. It was a huge loss for us all.

My dad had been the head of the family. He was always the one with the good advice. He did everything, except looking after the home, which was my mum's domain. He looked after all the money, the bills, the garden, the heavy work, and the DIY. My mum was completely panic-stricken when we told her Dad wasn't going to live. She was in a terrible state and we had to call an ambulance as we thought she was having a heart attack. After that, my mum needed looking after, and we bought a bungalow next to her so that we could see her all the time. She has been with me for all our meals ever since.

Dad was always my go-to person. Always part of the solution whenever anything went wrong. I knew he would be able to help me sort out any problem. Everyone looks to me now, as I have turned into him. But I am lost without him.

James and Abigail greatly miss their Grandad Ted to this day.

A FABULOUS MUM

With Mum's Christian faith, I grew up knowing that the Everlasting Arms are underneath you, and round about you, so you will never hit rock bottom. It's what I have always learned and that is how my family have always lived.

She doesn't like all the touchy-feely things of today. She thinks that people should pull themselves together more, and that sometimes you have got to just get on with it. She says, 'Onwards and upwards!'

That said, my mum was always so good to talk to. When I was young and crying of a broken heart, she would say, 'Look, I know you don't think this now, but you won't remember his name next week, promise.' She was right. She was really good with comforting me and she was a lovely mum. She's just so sweet-natured, and my grandparents were the same, whereas my dad had a right temper like me!

My mum has always been in my corner, always there, whatever has gone on in my life. She has been a fabulous mum. The best, honestly.

LOOKING BACK

I don't look back now. I look forwards. For instance, when different members of my family died, and since my dad died, I have never been able to go to Cornwall or to Devon, as I find it too emotional. I am not one to give in to emotions much. I only cried about five years after my dad died, when we had to empty his garage, taking all his tools out, when my mum moved bungalows. It makes me emotional to think of it even now.

Helping with this book has inevitably meant I had to look back, which has been unusual for me. It's forced me to go out of my comfort zone and face emotions. But remembering all of this only strengthens my knowledge of what a very lucky girl I was to have my mum and dad as parents. I had an idyllic childhood.

Nan and Grand

BY ABIGAIL HORNE

Ask me to remember my childhood and I'll think of times spent with my grandparents. I'm sure James, my elder brother, feels exactly the same.

We spent every weekend sleeping over with Nan and Grand and didn't want to go home on a Sunday. It wasn't that life with our parents was bad in any way, just that life with Nana and Grandad was everything you could want a life with grandparents to be – fewer rules and more fun!

James and I only knew a life in which Nan and Grand played a major part. They were hugely involved in our upbringing, and they couldn't have been any more supportive or more fun to be around. We got away with murder, as you can imagine.

We both feel so lucky to have had this childhood, looking back.

A CHILDHOOD WITH OUR GRANDPARENTS

We called our grandad Grand. One of those painful memories that has stuck in my mind is that my brother organised a massive flower arrangement for his funeral that just said 'Grand'. For James and me, they have always been Nan and Grand, even though, since losing Grandad, my nan now refers to herself as Nanny P.

I think of all the birthday and Christmas cards they gave us over the years, and every card was always signed from 'Nan and Grand'. Then when my grandad died, I think there must have been a moment when Nan wasn't sure how to sign off the cards anymore, so she changed it to Nanny P. The great-grandchildren have only ever known her as Nanny P – none of them met my grandad.

I remember Nan and Grand's house very well. My grandad practically built it. He was constantly adding to it, always working on it, and so the house was never without a project going on. It just seemed to keep getting bigger and better.

James and I only really knew that house. It was more important than the house we lived in with our parents. It feels so sad that it isn't my nan's house anymore. I loved it so much that I wanted to buy it, but it wasn't the right time.

I can still remember the distinctive, patterned Axminster that ran through the house and the smell of Nan cooking Sunday dinners. Sunday dinner was always a big meal, served at noon sharp. Actually, I can recall what that house smelt like on any day of the week. We always knew what meal was coming. My grandparents were very regimented with food - perhaps that is just a grandparent thing - but each day of the week had its own meal, with Fishy on a Dishy on a Friday. My favourite was Nan's chips, peas and eggs which we enjoyed on a Saturday night. Grandad was all about mashed potato sandwiches, which was standard lunch for most of our childhood.

Those meals were important to us because my grandad picked us up from school every day, looking after us until my mum finished work, so we had our tea there every single night, as well as the weekends, of course.

My grandad was a funny one. When he collected us from school, he would either be in a mood that I was late coming out or he would be ready to tell me all the things he had read in the news-paper that would affect my life. He was like the bearer of bad news, all the time. We would call him a pessimist, and he would say, 'I'm not a pessimist, I'm a realist!'

Don't get me wrong, I loved my time with Grandad. But I found the best way to deal with those car journeys from school was to avoid conversations by having a CD on. We listened to more Lionel Richie in that car than anywhere else.

My grandad retired early, whereas Nan worked until she was sixty. That meant Grandad didn't just pick us up from school during term times, but he looked after us for six weeks in the school holidays. It makes me laugh now, that for those six weeks he fed James and me mashed potatoes sandwiches every day. They were terrible, with the skin still on the potatoes. But if you asked us what we missed the most now, it would be eating those skin-on mashed potato sandwiches!

During our school holidays, he packed a stripy bag with a big bottle of water in it, and some of those crappy sandwiches, and sent James and me to the park. We spent all morning at a local Play Scheme, coming back for a bit of dinner and then going back to the park in the afternoon. That was pretty much how we spent the six-week holidays. Nowadays, of course, you would never let your kids do that, but it was a reasonably safe thing to do back then. Life was just a little different, and the outside world felt a bit safer.

On a Friday and Saturday night, when we stayed at Nan and Grand's house, my brother had a bedroom in the loft, and I had the other bedroom overlooking the back garden. When Grandad used to go to the pub, where he loved playing darts with his friends, my nan would let us stay up till just before he was due to come home, around midnight. Their lives were very regimental, with dinners and most things happening at the same times - you could set a watch by our life - so Nan would know exactly when Grandad was five minutes away from walking through the gates. She would turn to us and say, 'Quick! Get in bed. You've got to pretend you've been there since eight o'clock!'

We ran back to our bedrooms so as not to get her in trouble. She was so much fun, and she still is so much fun.

With my grandad as the authority figure, Nan was - and is - this earth angel that allowed us to do anything we wanted. She let us have all the mint chocolate ice creams we wanted and let us have so much fun.

Nan was also very caring, and she used to read to us every night. Books were a massive part of our bedtime routine (there are too many to mention!). She would sing to us every single night, especially one song called 'I Delight', a Christian song from church. At bedtimes, Nan prayed, as she is very much a Christian woman.

My grandad was really hands-on. If there was ever a little bit of snow, we would be outside building a snowman and he would be playing with us. He also used to film us all the time, which means our whole childhood is captured on videotapes.

We played so many games with Nan and Grand. They never begrudged us staying there. They wanted us there all the time, and we wanted to be there all the time too.

GRANNY'S GROTTY GROTTO

We have many happy memories of Christmas time at Nan and Grand's house. We had our Christmas dinners there, and I will never forget how my nan turned the house into Santa's Grotto. Imagine the most tinsel you have ever seen in all your life, with homemade tin foil and plastic Christmas decorations on the tree. That was their house at Christmas. We used to call it Granny's Grotty Grotto. It wasn't like those perfect, Instagrammable Christmas photos you see, but to us, it was Christmas at Nan and Grand's house, and it was perfect.

Nana was so creative; she was crafty with so many things. Lots of our toys were homemade, including my doll's house. She also made all our clothes, and James and I were always made to wear matching outfits; my dress would match my brother's shirt! She was an avid sewer. Come to think of it, I think she made my First Holy Communion dress too. I haven't seen her sew for years now, but it was a skill that she passed on to Becky, my brother's wife, who is also a very good sewer. Nan gave her sewing machine to Becky, so it has not been lost from the family.

SPECIAL HOLIDAYS

Torcross in Devon needs a special mention. My mum and dad, Nan and Grand, and James and I went there every single year until I was a teenager, staying in Torcross Hotel, Slapton Sands.

The journey there was always eventful. My brother always went with my mum and dad, as he knew the journey would pass a lot quicker. I would end up having to go with Nan and Grand.

The only way to describe my grandad's driving is that he was filled with road rage and anxiety. My nan would take a travel sickness pill which had the side effect of making her act like a daft, drunk person in the front of the car, trying to read a map for my angry grandad. I remember Nan used to keep a wet cloth in a pencil case resembling a Walker's salt and vinegar crisp packet. Grandad used to get so angry with her for not being able to read the map, that she would take this cloth out and dab it on my grandad's forehead as he was driving. My brother and my parents would get down to Devon in four hours. After twelve hours we would still be driving around in circles. These are the things I remember fondly.

Another funny thing I remember is how my grandparents were so set in their ways with food and routine, that there was a book where Grandad used to write down all the things they needed to take on holiday with them. Grandad liked fruit at five o'clock, so the fruit bowls came down with us. He liked braised steak and chips cooked a certain way, and so my nan would have to pack the pressure cooker. The book had page after page of things for my nana to pack that nobody would normally take on holiday with them. All so that my grandad could stay in his routine. This made our lives on holiday a continuation of our daily lives, as everything had to stay the same. They were that set in their ways. Well, Grand certainly was.

In Torcross, we spent the whole day with my grandparents playing on the beach. Those holidays were the best of our lives. We would do all the simple things that we take for granted now that we have phones and the internet.

Fishing formed a big part of our holidays. We used to fish all day and caught mackerel that Grandad would teach us to stun, kill, gut and cook. So, we often caught our own tea or breakfast, depending on when we chose to eat the catch of the day. Thinking about it, it was a bit gruesome, but I didn't know any different. My mum would always get annoyed because she would put me in my lovely dress for the evening and do my hair in a pretty way, ready for the "games room" at night time, and then I would run straight down to the beach where my grandad was still fishing, and I would get covered in fish guts and blood.

When you lose someone close to you, places and memories become all you have left, and Torcross is one of those places for me. We don't stay there now, as the hotel isn't open anymore, but James and I still take our own children there every year, to play on the beach and carry on the holiday traditions.

There is a picture of Grandad and me sitting on a blanket on that pebble beach, which sums up everything that I remember about my childhood.

A SOURCE OF COMFORT AND SUPPORT

My mum remembers that my nan was very conscious of her looks and appearance, and always wanted to be part of the glam squad, but that is a nana from a different era. I met my nan at a time when her life became purely about the grandchildren.

My husband, Aarran, always comments on how there is no one quite like my nan on earth. He says she is just the most beautiful person he has ever known, inside and out, and I believe it. She really is like an earth angel. It's said that everyone has good and bad in them but there is not a bad bone in her body. She is pure love all the way through. Selfless love. This is the nana I have known.

When I was going through challenging times growing up, I would go to my nan. I wouldn't go to my grandad. He wasn't someone you would go to for sympathy. He was tough as old boots. The most I would ever get from him was a pat on the head for comfort, whereas my nan was the ultimate comfort machine. She just wanted to wrap you in a blanket and make everything better.

I experienced a lot of bullying at school, and my nan was such great support. She would never suggest that I could have done anything wrong myself. She would immediately have my back. Nan always made me believe that none of the things I was being targeted for were my fault.

'It's because you're beautiful, and it's because you're clever,' she would say.

She always took the opportunity to make me feel like a million dollars, to help me understand that none of it was me, and none of it was the result of something I needed to change about myself. She was just so protective of me.

With my nan, it is not so much the things she says but the things she does. She's one for brushing things off, so if I was upset or was having a hard time, she would say, 'We're not going to think about that, because that's miserable, and we're going to have some fun. We're going to watch our favourite film and I'm going to put this blanket around you.' She is still like this now.

My nan is so loving, whereas my grandad was always very practical. My first job was a paper round, and to support me Grandad delivered my papers with me every day. In fact, at one point I just gave up on the paper round because I hated it and he ended up doing it for me. I am sure he was the oldest paperboy in the Midlands!

FUN TIMES

When James and I were naughty – often James, when he broke something and blamed me – it would be me who got in trouble even though we all knew it was him. He was (and still is) the golden boy.

James could be quite, how do I put it... not well behaved. My nana used to have a cup of tea with rich tea biscuits. She used to dip two of them in together, eating them like a sandwich. One time, James stuck chewing gum between her biscuits before

Nana dipped them in her tea. The chewing gum melted, and she could feel the chewing gum inside her for weeks!

If we were really bad, Nan or Grand locked us in separate bedrooms and removed the locks so we couldn't get out. We had to stay there until we had calmed down and learnt how to behave. I remember how James and I talked through the walls, trying to work out an escape. It's so funny to think about it now.

As a teenager, James and his friends were young lads up to naughty things, as young lads do. You would think my nana, who was becoming elderly, would have been frightened of these lads. After all, other people in the area crossed the street to avoid them. But Nan would be giving them all a cup of tea in her living room. They cherished and adored her, calling her Nanny P, as my friends do as well. She has this way about her that makes you want to do anything for her.

There is one thing that happened with my nan that was hilarious. Nan has always enjoyed buying clothes from charity shops. One time, she bought a pair of chequered green trousers, exactly like the trousers in the music video for Outcast's song, *Hey Ya!*. One day Nan and I – Nan wearing these trousers – were walking up the bank to get back home and a car full of teenage lads pulled up next to us. They wound the windows down and started singing *Hey Ya!*, doing the dance movements too. My nan stood there laughing, dancing and singing it back at them. She is just hilarious. Every time I hear that song it reminds me of that moment. I will never forget it.

FLOWERS AND FRESH AIR

I can't finish without mentioning that my nana is – or was when she was more able – a keen gardener. Their bungalow was known for its beauty. She wanted it to be the most beautiful house on the road. She wanted everyone to be envious of their flowers, and she and my grandad worked relentlessly to make sure their whole bungalow looked like the Chelsea Flower Show.

We haven't had the inclination ourselves to make our gardens like that, so I wouldn't say the skill of gardening passed down to anyone. But both James and I have created incredible spaces outside for our children to spend time in and grow up in . After all, when we were growing up, we were always outdoors. That's the way it was. If you were cold, you were brought a cup of tea outside. We grew up away from screens. This is why I am the way I am, creating a culture where our children are outside, come rain, shine, or freezing cold. I want them in the garden getting fresh air.

GONE FISHING: REMEMBERING GRAND

I have a wonderful dad that I've got an amazing relationship with, but my grandad was a different sort of dad to me. He was my biggest strength.

Some people may have thought that he could come across as a bit difficult, but to me, he wasn't. He is all of my happy memories. He is all of *our* happy memories, and I speak on behalf of James as well. The hardest thing I've ever been through was losing him because he was such a big character for us. He was so important to me that when I found out I was pregnant, just three months after he died, we named our son Ted after him.

James and my grandad were very close, father and son close.
Their relationship was like mine with my nan. They were best
friends. They bonded through fishing, which they spent their
life doing together. It was their thing. I did a lot of fishing too
when I was little, when we used to catch fish on Torcross beach,

but my brother and grandad took that a lot further. They got fishing passes to many places in the local area, so they would fish on lakes around here. It was such a big part of my brother's life.

The thing I remember most about my grandad, aside from fishing, is that he was the most incredible darts player. I remember him sitting, even when we were watching TV in the living room, constantly practising his throw with his hand. We have hundreds and hundreds of his trophies. And every year we used to have a holiday down to Devon Cliffs because he would win it for us at the darts championships.

Darts is incredibly special for us all now. Every Christmas we watch the darts, not because I care who wins, but because it reminds me of him. Darts and fishing are also huge for my nan, as special reminders of Ted.

Something that comes to my mind when I think of the moments I have shared with Grandad, is when he went into remission from his lymphoma. Suddenly, we could talk with him about things we hadn't been able to when we didn't know if he'd make it or not – which, of course, sadly he didn't in the end. But there was a moment, before he got ill again, when I said to him, 'You've been given a second chance, Grandad. What are you going to do differently?'

'I'm not going to do anything differently,' he replied. 'I'm going to live this happy life with your nana every single day like I've been doing for the last fifty years because she's every bit of happiness that I've ever wanted.'

Imagine getting over cancer and being given a second chance, and yet realising you wouldn't change a thing about your life. That moment was really special to me, particularly when I think about it now. I know that even if he was here, he wouldn't have done anything any differently.

It hurts me every day that my grandad never got to see the good bits in my life and James's life. He got to see the teenage bits, the relationships that went wrong, the house moves. He didn't get to see us getting married or settling down and having children. My nana has been able to enjoy all of that, despite an inevitable sadness that will always live in her, after losing a husband of fifty years. But she has found joy. We have given her joy.

UNBREAKABLE BONDS

As a family, we are always together.

The relationship my nan has with my brother is a bond like no other. James is Nan's golden boy. As the first baby boy in the family, he was everything my nan and grandad ever wanted. James was the most special thing to them in the world. My brother had a special relationship with both of them.

I was cherished by them too, of course, and my nan and I are best friends. I cannot explain the relationship with my nan. It is something you would have with a best friend your own age. People might wonder how a thirty-five-year-old and eighty-one-year-old do the things that we do together, but we do. She is always my person of choice, and I would rather do something with her than anyone. Our relationship even has a following on social media. People love Nanny P!

When I say that my nana and I are best friends, I mean that we have spent my thirty-five years laughing and doing the most ridiculous things. Only a few years ago, when my son Ted was about four, I bought a hoverboard. Nanny P was seventy-five and whipping around the house on it!

Then, of course, there is the relationship between my mum and nan. We are all so close as a family.

When my grandad died, Mum and I bought properties together on the same road near my nan. We came together in the most painful time in our lives. I lived there until I had my second child and outgrew the house, but my mum and nan still live next to each other. And my mum brings Nan up to us a couple of mornings a week to be with the kids. There are so many things we still do together that I can't think of one specific thing that stands out, as she's just such a huge part of our lives.

There are a million happy memories with her: every Friday night when she let us watch films that we shouldn't have been watching; when she let us stay up late when we shouldn't have been; every holiday playing with kites on the beach; letting us have way more mint chocolate ice creams than we were allowed; playing ping pong together every evening in the clubhouse on holidays, as she wasn't bothered about being with the adults, being always just for us. I am just so lucky. My nan and grandad are every bit of happiness I have ever known.

From childhood, through our teenage years, and up to where we are now, James and I have been going to visit my nan most days our whole lives. Now we don't go over for meals anymore, as she tends to have her meals at my mum's, but we just scoop her up and involve her in what we're doing. If I'm going shopping, I just grab her, and she comes with me. If my brother's going to the theatre, he takes her with him. If we are booking a holiday in this country, we take her with us.

NANNY P AND THE GREAT-GRANDKIDS

Nanny P is everything to everyone, including all her great-grandkids.

I have three kids now. My eldest, Ted, is ten years old, Polly is three years old, and Bobby is seventeen months. Then there's my brother's daughter, Grace, who is six years old. Our kids have brought so much joy to our family.

My son, Ted, the first great grandchild, came in the hardest of times, as he was born soon after my grandad died. Nana would say he saved her life. He gave her something to live for, a reason to be here, especially when all those hard anniversaries and Christmas came along in that first year. Grandad Ted was not replaced, but we had Baby Ted to do all those things with instead. He was really important to my nan, and I feel that a big part of my grandad lives on in my son, Ted, even though he's too young to realise all of this.

EAT THE CAKE: WISDOM THROUGH THE GENERATIONS

My mum's an amazing person, but often thinks me and my nan get up to most ridiculous things and eye rolls at us. She has playfully called us, 'A pair of idiots together' on more than one occasion. Double trouble if you like.

She is more like my grandad in personality, liking everything neat, tidy, and clean. My nan and I have always lived by the rule, 'You only live once!'

We don't sweat any of the small things. We live life to its absolute fullest.

During the Covid-19 pandemic, you couldn't keep my nan in. Whatever is going on in the world, she thinks, 'If that's how I'm going to go, then I'm going to go out having a laugh!'

On her eightieth birthday, I asked her, 'What advice or wisdom would you give me from your eighty years?'

Her reply says it all.

'Don't bother cleaning up, it's a waste of your life. And eat all the cake.'

She doesn't worry about anything. She just eats the cake.

We don't sweat the small stuff.

Just enjoy.

Enjoy it all.